I0829817

REFRAME: THE MAGAZINE FOR PROFESSIONAL HYPNOTISTS

A PUBLICATION OF THE ICBCH, INC.

DR. RICHARD K. NONGARD
EXECUTIVE DIRECTOR

Editor in Chief
CHRISTINA MATTHEWS, LCPC

Associate Editor
RICHARD DAMA, LPC

CONTENTS

FROM THE PRESIDENT'S DESK

DR. RICHARD K. NONGARD

THE ICBCH IS a non-profit educational organization devoted to training hypnotists, providing member services and educating the public. We are governed by a board of advisors who all hold the idea that hypnosis should be collaborative and open to all. The research is clear, hypnosis is not a "complementary and alternative" modality, it is a first line intervention that can change lives.

This magazine is published as a resource for professional hypnotists. It is a combination of both scholarly articles, and personal experiences and applications that the authors have shared. We appreciate their efforts and hope you enjoy what they have written.

The ICBCH holds an annual convention in February of each year. The 2019 ICBCH and HPTI Winter HypnoConference will be held February 25-27, 2019 in sunny Las Vegas. We hope you join us for a learning experience celebrating those who are passionate about helping others with professional hypnosis.

For more information
call our office at (702) 418-3332 or visit
https://hypnosistraininginstitute.org/hpti-winter-hypnosis-convention/.

The Big News!

After many months of effort, the ICBCH is now able to provide its members with a group health care plan. This means if you are a current member of the ICBCH you can apply for coverage for you and your family (United States only). ICBCH instructor Jeffrey Richards played a big role in helping us secure this membership benefit and we appreciate his efforts to make this a reality.

ICBCH members are also able to purchase professional liability insurance as practicing hypnotists who are seeing clients either part-time or full-time. Please contact our office to find out how you can get coverage for your professional needs.

Reframe Magazine

This magazine is our new publication which supersedes our newsletter. It is available online for all ICBCH members. Editor-in-Chief, Christina Matthews, LCPC and Associate Editor Richard Dama, LPC have tirelessly edited these pages. The ICBCH board wants to thank them for their efforts.

To submit an article for the next edition, email richard@hypnosisnevada.com.

Are you a member of the ICBCH?

To support our professional efforts and access the many member benefits, you can join by taking an approved training course or join through reciprocity. We recognize your previous training, and if you are a certified member of another organization you can also join the ICBCH. You can find reciprocity information or a directory of approved trainers at hypnotherapyboard.com.

I am looking forward to seeing you at our upcoming conference in February. Make sure you register now to get the early-bird rate and the discounted hotel rooms at the Orleans Hotel in Las Vegas.

Best Wishes,
Dr. Richard Nongard, 2018-2019 ICBCH President

THE NEXT STEP!

Now that you have saved your seat, get your hotel reservations! The
Orleans is offering the first 100 to book room nights a special discount
of $46 per night (plus mandatory resort fee). The Orleans Hotel and

Casino is a landmark hotel in Las Vegas. It is conveniently located near the south end of Las Vegas Blvd. but just off the strip at 4500 W Tropicana Ave. For Reservations call (800) 675-3267 or Register online at https://www.orleanscasino.com/groups and use **group code: A9HWC02**. The Group name is: HPTI Winter Conference. All travel, lodging and meals expenses are the responsibility of attendee and are not included in conference registration/tuition fees.

Questions? Call (918) 236-6116 to Register by Phone or visit HPTI.org to Register Online

UNIFIED HYPNOSIS

CHRISTINA MATTHEWS, MS MA LCPC CCHI, EDITOR IN CHIEF

"HELLO AND WELCOME ABOARD" **as our Founder, Dr. Richard Nongard** always says when he begins any teaching session whether live or in person.

I am pleased to be a part of **ICBCH and HPTI** as a Certified Instructor and as a newly appointed Editor of Research. I practice clinical counseling and hypnosis in the Western Suburbs of Chicago, focusing on clients with trauma and PTSD, and, as a long-time teacher, I also work with students to gain academic success. I hope as you read the articles submitted by our members, you will be enlightened, educated, and inspired. We have outstanding members whose skills are as unique as they are vast. Participating in the **ICBCH and HPTI** social media forums, posts, online and recorded classes, and training events will be an excellent use of your time and help you expand your knowledge base and professional abilities while simultaneously meeting and befriending amazing new colleagues. Additionally, I hope you will take time to **submit your own articles** and share your unique skills and insights with all of us.

As you will notice, some of the submissions are very scholarly with cited references from meta-searches. Other articles are practical in nature, sharing specific techniques and insights from niches in private practices. Both are most welcome! We want to hear from you!

ICBCH and HPTI are embarking on a new journey to raise the standards of competency and capability of its members. This is the time for a call to unity in our profession and establish our organizations as the benchmark of professional excellence for Hypnosis and Hypnotherapy world-wide. We need to consider levels of unity in our c, and even within ourselves.

Standards

Within any profession entrusted to serving the public, there must be unified guidelines to protect the safety of our clients. Currently, there are many schools of thought on what can be considered a competent and capable hypnotist/hypnotherapist. It would be wise for our own community to use consultation to come together to decide on benchmarks that reflect knowledge, experience, and awareness of individual client needs before we end up having a higher authority outside our field make these decisions for us as they have been made in most all other service professions, i.e., medicine, counseling/social work, teaching, etc.

Relationships

ICBCH and HPTI are organizations rich in strong bonds within their communities. Members enjoy social and professional contact and find meaningful friends and colleagues. Still, within these memberships, individual school of thought exist. There are times when forum discussions include derisive comments about the value of another's individual credentials or usefulness in the field. To be unified, we must first realize our internal maps will most likely not match those of anyone else as closely as we may think. It is important to listen and consider the perspective of each person. By considering new viewpoints and being able to see, hear, feel what the other side sees, feels, hears, we may be able to open up new dialogues, learn new information, and use what is gained to form a knowledge base that can impact decisions and directions for our field in a positive way. Everyone contributes knowledge and expertise that is vital to the field of hypnosis/hypnotherapy. By communicating respectfully and learning what we hear, we all will improve our skills and become even more competent professionals.

Resources

ICBCH and HPTI offer resources that are second to none. I just noticed that the NBCC and APA are starting to offer online convention-type webinars. Our organizations are ahead of the curve with techniques to keep us connected and educated. The recent Online Hypnosis Convention provided top-ranked speakers and their video and print resources for us to use over and over. Members are continually posting new ideas and links to information in the forums and on their own personal websites, video channels, Facebook forums, and other social media sources. By teaching each other through sharing our resources, we can bring this profession to a whole new level!

Personal Unity

While extremely urgent that we become unified in standards, relationships, and resources, the most important place for unity is within our own selves. We must be aware that our successful results depend on our own inner awareness. As NLP teaches, to create success, we must examine our behaviors, skills, abilities, beliefs (both limiting and empowering) and values/motivations. We may be extremely skillful but have no results, so we must look inward to decide where we need to make changes. Are our goals and values aligned? Perhaps our changes need to be a willingness to take on the perspectives of others. Or, until we try to make changes in our mindset and actions, we might not even be aware we have limiting beliefs or negative emotions that are getting in the way.

Whatever the case, as we all become part of something new and exciting and are willing to become agents of change for a unified field (quantum reference intentional) of Hypnosis and Hypnotherapy can become even more fantastic than the one we now know.

I am excited to continually meet new friends among the ranks of the famous, the scholarly, the practical, and the innovators. I look forward to expanding my colleague and friend base and definitely look forward to the contributions you all make to our organizations.

Looking forward to meeting you at the HPTI Convention in February 2019!

MYTH OF THE RESISTANT CLIENT

KELLEY T. WOODS

MODERN HYPNOSIS (the evolution of hypnotherapy within the last ten or so years) has been moving away from several limiting beliefs around how to help clients with hypnosis. Mindsets and language of controlling a client, measuring "susceptibility", and otherwise putting the bulk of the responsibility of success upon someone other than the hypnosis practitioner have fallen out of favor.

One of the most outdated constructs within the hypnosis field is the idea of a resistant client. A resistant client may be defined as a client who does not respond to efforts by the hypnotist to induce a hypnotic trance. This description is problematic to begin with, since hypnotic states have not been scientifically quantified. More modern practitioners, in fact, are identifying with the idea that people are in constant "trance" states, whether they are stuck in eating trances, pain trances, depression trances, etc., and it's more a matter of determining whether said trances are helpful, or not.

In less-evolved certification courses, students are taught that if a client is not responding to a process that they are "resisting" – by failing to keep eyes closed, raise an arm or otherwise exhibit hypnotic phenomena. This can also be the reason given when a client doesn't experience desired change following a hypnosis session. The belief is that these people are consciously or unconsciously refusing to comply due to:

1. fear
2. stubbornness
3. "secondary gain"

The truth is that any client who has bothered to book an appointment with a hypnosis practitioner, shows up on time and is prepared to pay the fee is hardly resistant. Especially for those who have suffered chronic issues such as pain, anxiety or other debilitating problems, the desire for relief and improvement is immense. They are arriving with a high degree of hope and even some belief that what is going to happen will help them.

It is the hypnosis practitioner's charge to be adept at determining what approach will be best for the client. Less experienced hypnotists who have received training that is limited to a single "protocol" may be challenged in doing that. Because people are different, it is vital to have a wide variety of approaches on hand to find the right one for any client.

In many cases, if an approach is not effective and the client is not responding to it, the problem may be one of the following:

1. The hypnotist did a poor job of discovering what the client expects
2. The hypnotist did not utilize what a client revealed
3. The hypnotist is attempting to make the client fit the approach
4. The hypnotist is not skilled or confident in executing the approach
5. There is a lack of rapport
6. The client is simply not following directions

Some of the above can be avoided with a well-conducted pretalk. Old School training suggests that a hypnotist reassure a client of many "nots" – that they will not become stuck in hypnosis, that they will not reveal deep secrets, that they will not be controlled in any way. This is a self-defeating process: why suggest these things to people who may not have even worried about them?! A more helpful tactic is to, near the end of the pretalk, simply ask, "Do you have any questions or concerns?"

What IS important to do during a pretalk is to elicit information that can be utilized. This requires the art of effective listening; active listening is a skill that allows the hypnotist to isolate salient points that can be later used for the client's benefit. These may pertain to previous experiences and attempts to solve the presenting issue, motivation for improvement, personal preferences, strengths and weaknesses, etc.

By paying attention and encouraging a client to cultivate deeper awareness of their challenges along with their successes, these details easily surface. The adroit hypnotist will then have plenty of fodder to not only use for hypnotic suggestions, they will have a clear direction of what technique or approach to use with the client.

Sometimes, the problem is that a practitioner over-complicates things. It's easy to overestimate a new client's ability to comprehend what is being offered; using industry language that is familiar to a hypnotist can sound foreign to a layperson. Many NLP processes contain several steps and explaining them to a client who is already stressed and not in the best learning state can sabotage responsiveness.

The solution for this is to keep things simple. Introduce only one or two new ideas or techniques in a session. Ask yourself: is this a person who wants to know the details of why a process works? They may be and breaking it down for them can help them engage even better but, if the client doesn't care about that, over-explaining will only frustrate and confuse them. Read your client and respond appropriately for who they are.

Conversely, some new hypnotists have observed the ease and finesse by which seasoned experts "drop" a person into hypnosis. They are then dismayed when it doesn't work for them and revert to the resistant client frame. It's important to realize that creating expectation and belief is probably one of the most important tasks – to inspire a client so that by the time the hypnotic ritual happens, they can't wait to experience it! Imagine being invited to a party...you are at the front door and you hear the laughter, the music, the clinking of glasses. You are a bit nervous (excited) because you don't know exactly what is going to happen when the door finally opens and you are invited in. That's the feeling a client needs to engage in hypnosis!

Now, even an experienced hypnotist will occasionally meet a client who isn't as responsive as they hoped. This certainly happens but the difference here is that the well-versed hypnotist will never blame this on the client. Instead, they will dip into their vast bucket of tools and pull out another. Rarely, there will be a client who just isn't a good fit for hypnosis and in this case, honesty is the best policy.

A common roadblock, as mentioned earlier, arrives when a hypnosis practitioner is wedded to a certain protocol. They wholeheartedly believe that it is THE best and that it can solve any person's problem. This narrow viewpoint can only eventually result in two things:

1) The practitioner's skills are limited to that one approach and therefore limiting them to further growth

2) There is a risk to a client when the practitioner refuses to acknowledge that it's not the client who is the resistant one

There have even been unfortunate cases of clients being subjected to a type of psychological force-feeding, an insistence that if they will only stop resisting, things will work. In some of these cases, other hypnotists from the same school of thought have been brought in to further gang up on a client, causing even more damage! This has occurred to the degree that clients have been told that they must have "sold their soul to the devil", since they are so resistant to the approach. This, obviously, is extremely abusive, unethical and contrary to professional hypnosis practice.

The solution to situations like the above is education. Every hypnosis certification course needs to drop frames such as "resistance" and embrace principles of active listening, utilization and other client-centered approaches. Hypnotists should have plenty of opportunities to practice the intake and pretalk process, executing convincers and inductions, and have a sound grasp of the power of influence. While working with clients can, and often should, take a light-hearted approach, it is also a great responsibility.

Hypnosis clients deserve to receive informed, ethical and compassionate service. For the earnest hypnosis practitioner, this means taking training that is current, being well-practiced, and operating from a perspective of finding the best approach for every client.

HIRE STAFF TO SCALE UP YOUR HYPNOSIS BUSINESS

JASON LINETT

THIS IS the kind of problem you want. Your schedule is maxed out for the next few weeks. Potential clients are showing appropriate signs of frustration that they have to wait to see you. If a client needs to reschedule, they're surprised to learn it'll be a few weeks before they can get in again.

It's time to scale up your business, and consider hiring additional staff. I will share some of the mindsets and strategies I've personally used over the years at my Virginia Hypnosis office to take on additional practitioners.

We must first address "Superhero Syndrome." This mindset holds back many business owners, not just hypnotists. It's the belief that no one can do the work as good as you do. Yes, you're an outstanding hypnotist with phenomenal skills. I'd encourage you to step into an "instructor's mindset" and discover your skills are transferable.

Find a practitioner who already has a proven level of skill though perhaps doesn't have as much interest in running their own business. No matter their skill, acknowledge that some training on your behalf may be necessary. Consider offering their services specifically for one issue, like weight loss, fear release, stop smoking. As their confidence and efficacy rises, you can then expand their services.

Let's talk money. In my conversations with other practitioners, I've found the average to be that the staff member is paid around 30% to 50% of the session income. You have the greater overhead of office expenses, marketing, and administration, so this is very generous. As I've run my business, the hypnotist-on-staff doesn't have to handle anything beyond showing up wand working with clients. I handled the scheduling, phone consultations, and payments. As I agreed to take on the associate hypnotist, I made it a priority to fill their schedule before mine as they had committed their scheduled time.

How do you pay them? In the United States, it's common to have this person on staff as an independent contractor. They will be responsible for taxes due throughout the year. As my company is taxed as an "S Corporation," and I'm technically an employee of my own business. I'm on payroll for my company, so I've set my staff on payroll as well to automate the process and simplify the taxes. This will be a discussion to have with your staff member as well as your accountant.

When you have more people working with you, you not only scale up your business but also serve a larger local clientele to help more people. However, your potential client found YOUR website and has seen YOUR videos and fell in love with the idea of working with YOU. So how do you appropriately pivot this client to another practitioner?

Run your business with honesty, integrity, and transparency. Throw in a little creativity, and you are aimed for success. Here's how I've classically made the pivot.

I listen to the client. The process at Virginia Hypnosis begins with a free phone consultation which is really the first 5-10 minutes of an effective assessment of the client's goals. What would they like to change? How would they rather feel? What results do they want to notice immediately?

Once the foundation is in place, it's time to transition into the "Here's how we will work together" part of the phone call. I explain the program we'd recommend which details the number of sessions, the investment for the service, and any other related issues. Only as we're now deep in rapport and the commitment to the program is in place, I seamlessly make the pivot.

"Great, and I'll have you work with Stephanie on this as what she does best is help people naturally release anxiety and speak with confidence in public. Before getting into hypnosis, she had years of experience working as an educator. She brings this experience standing in front of thousands of students over the years into the hypnosis work she does here at Virginia Hypnosis. What time of day will work best for you next week either Tuesday or Wednesday?"

Timing, intention, and tonality are the key here. It's also paramount to build the perfect "because" as to why they will work with your staff member. In my experience, the rapport I've built with the client on the phone is easily transferred to the associate hypnotist.

Jason Linett is the host of the Work Smart Hypnosis podcast available online at www.WorkSmartHypnosis.com and the creator of www.HypnoticBusinessSystems.com, an incredibly comprehensive business training library for the modern hypnotist wishing to model success. He has built several six-figure hypnosis businesses, and shares this knowledge with you.

Jason will be sharing the stage with Dr. Richard Nongard during the first day of the HPTI and ICBCH HypnoConference in Las Vegas on February 25 to 27, 2019. Reserve your spot today at www.hypnosistraininginstitute.org/hpti-winter-hypnosis-convention.

DON'T GO IT ALONE

TRACY BARRETT ADAMS, CH.T.

HAVE you ever felt unsure of yourself in your hypnosis career? For even the most independent among us, launching a practice can have some slippery spots. So a helping hand from a colleague who's a little farther along the road can make all the difference in steady footing.

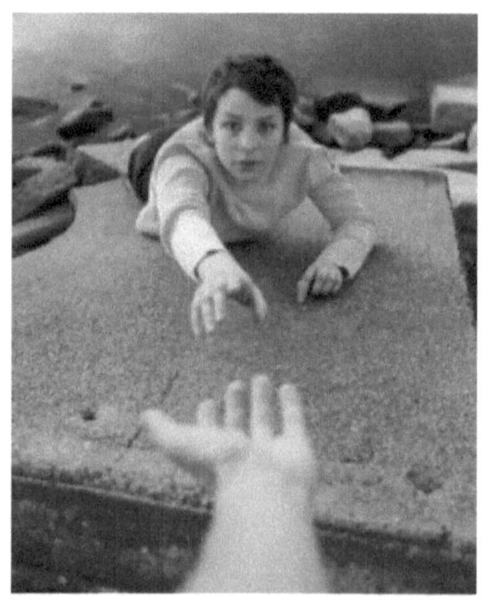

You probably already know that mentorship is valuable. Maybe you've been given the well-timed encouraging word by an insightful teacher, or a friend nudged you in the right direction. But did you know that the connection between ongoing mentorship and professional success is evidenced based? And studies show that it's a two-way street, with benefits for both mentees and mentors. [1][2]

As hypnosis practitioners, we're committed to helping our clients. And we're also managing a business, usually sorting it all out on our own. The good news is, help and community are available. So if you've felt frustrated in some areas of your practice, research tells us that having a mentor will probably help. Mentored professionals find their work more satisfying, feel more commitment and engagement in their work, and have a more optimistic belief system and expectancy about their future. [1]

And it's not surprising that so many practitioners love mentoring, because mentors also perceive feeling more satisfied and fulfilled in their careers, and many even report their roles as mentors make their lives feel more meaningful. [2]

Who Needs a Mentor?

Even the most accomplished professionals count on those they admire for encouragement and counsel. But it's the newer practitioners, or those who feel stalled, who will likely benefit most.

At every conference and on most forums, I meet practitioners who have trained (maybe multiple times), yet they still hesitate to cross into the field as a professional. It's probably a different story for each person. Certainly, it's easy to get stuck in the tricky paradox of feeling unready to take clients at the professional level until after we've already worked with several clients … at the professional level. For some it's a natural fear of the trapeze, swinging from old job to new career (often without a financial net), or maybe the daunting learning curves on areas like marketing, accounting, and websites.

We have wonderful online resources, forums and Facebook groups where practitioners can gather tips and share camaraderie, and it's tempting to use these groups as a kind of "hive mentor." As valuable as these platforms are, even in the most beautifully moderated forums, the very nature of these conversations means responses to your questions are from the framework of the responder, who can't adequately take into account your context, strengths, and challenges.

So there's benefit to looking beyond groups, to find personal connections that include active listening, rapport, and continuity. And nothing beats having someone you admire recognize more in you than you might have seen in yourself.

I discovered the value of mentorship in my first weeks as a hypnotherapist, shifting from a collaborative, team-based career to life as a solo-practitioner.

Armed with my crisp medical hypnosis certificate, a website, and the keys to my skyscraper office, I launched. What a thrill when my very first client called, a referral from my own doctor. This client had severe arthritis in both feet. I could hear the sadness in her voice, grieving her lost mobility and time spent doing things she'd loved, and she also expressed deep fear about the future.

Even as we talked, and my client became hopeful and excited about using hypnosis to reclaim her quality of life, a dense little cloud of doubt began to settle on my shoulders … *is this really going to help her?*

As the appointment approached I pored over my books and techniques, researching arthritis and reviewing scripts and protocols. Even so, that cloud got heavier, and moved toward the pit of my stomach … *what if she's disappointed?*

Though I was on the edge of canceling the appointment *(I'm not ready, it's too soon, it will be terrible)*, I remembered my favorite teacher had invited me to be in touch if I needed support. So I called, planning to get clarification on a pain relief technique.

As it turned out, we didn't talk about that technique. We had a conversation.

She reminded me about trusting the client to reveal what she needs in order to feel better. And she talked with me about hearing the client and responding. And most important, she expressed her conviction that this client would absolutely feel better for our work together. And so I breathed, and I kept the appointment (and … it went imperfectly perfect).

And this was the first of my many conversations with quite a few mentors. Some have worked with me in a peer-to-peer way, and others more formally on a paying basis. Every penny and every challenging conversation has been worthwhile.

How to Be a Great Mentee

Get over the fear of asking. Find a professional who is successful in the way that you want to be successful. Offer to pay for their time, it is probably valuable (and they may not charge you, but still, ask).

Be open to multiple mentors. For my part, the voices of Sherry Gilbert, Michael Ellner, and Kelley Woods formed a kind of chorus of encouragement and wisdom. Early in my career, their distinct points of view helped me find my own.

Use the time well. Whether or not you're paying for your mentoring sessions, consider yourself "on the clock." Though you might be friends with your mentor, do your part to keep these conversations focused and purposeful. Think ahead so you're ready to ask questions, and discuss your challenges and ideas.

Apply the lessons, and complete assignments. When your mentor suggests an action item, take action. Soon. This will make it easier for your mentor to offer perspective on progress, and work with you to you consider the steps to follow.

Ready to Mentor?

Yes, you do have something to offer. Even if you're fairly new and still getting established, you can reach right back behind you to support the student or new graduate. Remember, research shows those who mentor become more successful themselves. [2]

Give energy to listening. Bring an empathetic, solution-oriented mindset to these conversations. The cornerstones here are active listening, questions that reveal strengths and resources, and being present and thoughtful as you would with a hypnosis client.

Offer honest, kind feedback. Be transparent enough to help your mentee avoid some of your mistakes. And though you're obviously going to keep things constructive, don't shy away from honest insight and inviting conversations that will help your mentee stretch.

So Extend Your Hand

If you're feeling a little precarious or stuck in the mud, reach up for help. And if you're in a position to offer support, look for ways to do it. Whichever side of a mentoring relationship you're on, our whole profession becomes more grounded, and gains leverage to move forward from a position of strength.

----

[1] Allen TD, et al.; *J Appl Psychol.* 2004 Feb;89(1):127-36.
[2] Ghosh & Reio; *Journal of Vocational Behavior 83* (2013) 106–116
Photo by Noah Buscher on Unsplash

Tracy Barrett Adams specializes in working with pain, insomnia, neurological issues, childbirth, as well as healthy eating and body perception. She sees clients primarily through physician and licensed therapist referral. An IMDHA and ICBCH certified trainer, Tracy conducts one-on-one and group trainings for practitioner certification and medical hypnosis.

BULLETPROOF MOTIVATION

LEONARDO SILVÉRIO

I HAD a client who was trying to find motivation for dieting and exercising. The first time we met, I did some standard procedures to find values and thoughts that could move her in the right direction. What I did was to ask questions like "Why do you want to get more fit?" and "Imagine that you have already succeeded, so you are now in shape. How does your life change? What can you do now that you couldn't before? Why is this important?" and so on. The motivational ideas that came from this exercise were very useful.

After a few months, she met me again saying that she started very motivated. Everything was working perfectly, but then, she passed through stressful times due to some discussions with her father, and as a consequence, she stopped exercising and eating well. She told me things like "I remember that when we met before, I wanted to get in shape because I would feel confident with my self-image. And, that feeling more confident, I would work better, I would be happier in my relationship and so on." So, what has happened? She continued, saying "During that stressful episode, none of these thoughts made sense to me anymore. I didn't care if I was working out. I didn't care if my boyfriend desired me or not." "And right now, how do you feel?" I asked. "Now everything is fine, I do not feel stressed at all but I can't feel motivated to diet or exercise as I was before".

Not knowing exactly what I should do, I tried a different approach. It occurred to me that, sometimes, when I feel sad or angry, it seems that my priorities, that even my personal values, somehow change. What if "values and motivation are state-dependant?" So, thinking about that, I tried the following:

Step 1: I told her that ideas that make sense to us when we are in a state may not make sense when we are in a different state. "For instance, I am never aggressive. This is an important part of my values, but when I am playing soccer or even chess, I can play better when I desire to 'smash my opponent to the ground'. What I am saying is, that in sports, my values change and that this is OK. Do you know what I am saying?"

Step 2: I told her that we could do an exercise to find out which core values and thoughts could work to motivate her in any state, or, in other words, what could motivate her whether she was happy or sad and stressed. She accepted the idea.

Step 3: We started brainstorming any potentially motivating idea. We wrote down a long list of ideas, registering even those ideas that didn't feel motivational at all at first, like "I will have to buy new shoes and I like shopping."

Step 4: I asked her to close her eyes and told her that I would read out loud each of the items on our list. Her job was to tell me which idea felt more motivational and to give me a number between 0 and 10 corresponding to the intensity of the feeling. The result was very similar to what we got before: the search for confidence, leading to work and relationship improvement.

· · ·

Step 5: I asked her permission to elicit in her, momentarily, a state of stress and sadness. After her agreement, I asked her to close her eyes and to remember a time she felt bad or stressed. It could be the situation she had already mentioned - her fight with her father - or another one, even more stressful. I asked her to notice the feeling, give it a color and to keep it pulsing inside her body.

Step 6: With her in this state, I went through the same process of Step 4. In this part of the exercise, it was no surprise for me that the result was now different because she was in a very different mental and emotional state. In this 6th Step, the thought of being self-confident, working better and having a better relationship received a very low score! But one of the other motivational ideas stood out: the idea that, "if she gets in shape now, when she is older she will have a better health and she will be able to travel alone to other countries and so on." She told me later that she spontaneously remembered an old woman, in her 80's, that she saw traveling alone in Thailand when she was also traveling there, and remembered admiring her and thinking how amazing it would be to be that age and still have the energy for that.

Step 7: After breaking her state, I asked her if that idea was still motivational in a neutral state and she told that it was. So, I worked with her to make that thought even more powerful:

1. We did an exercise in her timeline, constructing a rich, colorful, and attractive image of her in the future being old and very healthy, travelling to many exotic countries. She would be a very sexy old lady.
2. I also gave her posthypnotic suggestions saying that, anytime she would think of not working out or not eating well, she would remember that old lady she will be, etc.

After one year, approximately, I spoke to her again and I was very pleased to know that she was doing very well, even though passing again through tough experiences which would have made her stop taking care of herself in the past.

When I think about this exercise we have done, I can point out that:

- Motivation and Hierarchy of Values can be state-dependant. Motivational thoughts which work with your client when they are happy may not make any sense when they are sad, and this may be the explanation for why people give up plans.
- We can trust ourselves to find motivational ideas that will work across many different states. I call them "bulletproof motivational ideas".
- The pretalk (Steps 1 and 2, mainly) sets a frame that suggests that you will find a more powerful motivation. I think that this frame works as a powerful indirect suggestion on itself.

RETHINKING CONFUSION

GRAHAM OLD

I WAS ORIGINALLY TAUGHT that the way to work with analytical clients, even resistant clients, was to confuse them. To speak in endless sentences, employing all kinds of clever language patterns, to wrap their mind up in trying to make sense of whatever I said. The idea was that they would get so confused that they would jump to accept the first meaningful thing that was said to them. If that meaningful thing was a suggestion to go into trance, into trance they would go!

I have to say that *can* work. However, after following this advice for many years, I have now come to the conclusion that it is a lousy way to treat people. Confusion inductions have never worked on me and I would be considered an 'analytical' client. I've always found them frustrating and it would seem that I am not the only one.

Questioning Confusion

In 2012, a study by the University of Notre Dame concluded that contrary to what we might presume, confusion *can* actually be beneficial to learning something, if – and this is important – *if* the confusion is ultimately resolved. Yet, what we often see with confusion inductions is the confusion being escaped from, *not* resolved.

Rather than being an experience to learn from, confusion becomes an annoyance to be avoided. Erickson records the reaction of one client:

'I have always felt somewhat annoyed and distressed by the Confusion Technique, and I have resented its use, but initially I was willing to listen and cooperate as best I could. Part of my resentment was undoubtedly due to my own mental pattern of thought; I always like to grasp each idea and organize my thoughts before proceeding. However, I went along with the confusion suggestions and I know they worked on me, although not as well as other techniques did.

At the present time they will not work on me. No matter how deep a trance I am in and how cooperative I am, I simply stop listening if that type of suggestion is begun. Nor will I make any pretence of listening. If the operator insists on keeping on talking, I shut off my hearing (self-established hypnotic deafness) and I may wake up feeling strongly annoyed.'

Research conducted by Stanger, Tucker & Morgan in 1996 found that confusion techniques were no more effective than a standard induction for low-susceptible subjects. Whilst it is unclear whether the low-susceptible subjects were analytical thinkers, it seems plausible to assume that at least some in that group would have been.

In 1985, Kirsch, Matthews and Mosher examined the 'double induction'. The procedure involves two hypnotists speaking into a subject's ears (one speaking to the left, one speaking to the right). This had been promoted by Bandler and Grinder as superior to traditional hypnotic inductions. Further, Lankton and Lankton claimed that using such two-level communication and interspersing suggestions in a confusing dual induction produces superior results. The researchers found no significant differences between the double induction and a traditional one in terms of depth of trance or response to suggestion. In fact, it seems that the double induction may actually *decrease* hypnotic responsiveness in some subjects!

How then do we account for the anecdotal evidence suggesting that confusion inductions work well, particularly for those with a more analytical thinking-style? There are a number of things to consider here.

Firstly, any anecdote that involves Erickson needs to be taken with a pinch of salt. This is not because they are necessarily inaccurate, but simply because he was Milton Erickson. After Erickson had reached a certain level of fame – often for using innovative hypnotic techniques – he was sought out by many for precisely that reason. Then, it seems fair to assume that the great doctor could have said anything to such visitors and they would have slipped into trance. When Erickson uttered confusing words it would have been a very clear signal that this was a hypnotic technique in action, prompting the expected response.

Secondly, some therapists turn to confusion techniques after having tried a number of other inductions unsuccessfully. It is certainly possible that by the time a confusion induction is employed, the client will have gone into and out of light trances enough times that any induction could have been used and effectively benefited from the previous fractionation.

Thirdly, confusion techniques certainly do work for some people. For example, Erickson records the experiences of two subjects:

'Miss H and Mr. T were excellent subjects for either traditional or the Confusion Techniques. However, after a few experiences with the Confusion Technique they reacted by bypassing it and developing a trance at once, no matter how subtly the author made his approach. As they would explain in the trance state, "As soon as I experienced the slightest feeling of confusion, I just dropped into a deep trance." They simply did not like to be confused. Neither of these subjects, fully capable with more common techniques, could seem to learn to use a Confusion Technique or even to outline a possible form. *There were others who responded similarly.*'

Practitioners of the confusion induction might celebrate this as an example of the induction actually working. After all, the clients bypassed the confusion and "dropped into a deep trance." However, note that 'they simply did not like to be confused.' This was not a pleasant experience for them. With such an experience, the induction becomes simply a tool to pressurise someone into trance. They gain nothing else from it. I hardly think this is an approach we should be promoting.

Using confusion to befuddle someone into trance is an outdated and non-therapeutic approach to inductions. I have no desire to cause someone to doubt themselves; quite the opposite. And I have no need to outsmart or out-analyse anyone. So, if someone has a strong and active mind, I want to help them use that to their advantage.

'Confusion techniques utilise whatever the client is doing to inhibit trance or other therapeutic developments *as the basis for inducing those developments.*'

I'm aware that my thoughts on confusion are in opposition to much of the writing on the subject. So, allow me to provide an example of the kind of client with whom I may still use some elements of confusion.

If someone comes to see me and they are an experienced meditator they may appear to be an ideal candidate for hypnosis. Without a doubt, they will be experienced at going in to trance and their interest in the process will produce an internal analytical loop that can be easily utilised. However, there can be a downside to such a client and that is their tendency to want to assist the hypnotist. If they want to analyse everything that it happening at the conscious and subconscious level, I have not got a problem with that and it makes my job substantially easier. Yet, if they are trying to fulfil my role, rather than allowing themselves to experience what is taking place, we could have difficulties. As such, I tend to say that I use confusion for people whose mind gets in their own way.

I strongly reject the outdated idea of using confusion to practically bully someone into submission. I find such a battle-of-the-wits idea to be unnecessary and unhelpful. In fact, it is a sure way to *increase* resistance and merely demonstrates that the hypnotist and the client are not on the same page. Instead, confusion is best employed as a temporary means of assisting clients to steer past an obstacle that they themselves desire to bypass.

So, I encourage my students to use confusion as part of their collaborative interaction with people, as an example of client-centred utilisation. That's almost the opposite to the battle-of-the-wits.

This may be the place to note that another reason why the battle of wits is unhelpful is that there is no guarantee that the hypnotist is going to win. If you do happen to be working with someone whose mind tends towards analysis, what makes you think that you are going to be able to stay one step ahead of them and confuse them into submission? They may very well keep up with everything you're saying and just end up annoyed at the nonsense you are wasting their time spouting.

***

Kinaesthetic Confusion

Of course, we should note that there is a difference between utilising confusion as an occasional technique and using it as the whole induction. Additionally, there are all sorts of ways that confusion can be employed. Linguistic confusion is but one example. Other types of confusion include:

- Unconscious/conscious dissociation
- Sensory overload
- Shifting states
- Kinaesthetic confusion
- And more...

I've talked about not using confusion to deal with so-called analyticals. However, I should mention that one of the main ways I *do* still use aspects of confusion is by employing kinaesthetic confusion. In doing so, I intentionally choose concrete memorable experiences versus confusing language. I know which I'd rather be on the receiving end of!

A good example of kinaesthetic confusion is seen in something like the Thain wrist-lift. The sudden catalepsy can create a moment of confused wonder and expectancy as your client receives the strong impression that the usual rules do not currently apply.

I like to think of inductions as "phenomenal learning experiences." Therefore, in my practice, the induction is an experiential learning process, with hypnotic phenomena at the core. A good example of this is something like the Elman Induction. This can function as a process for clients to partake in, not simply a passive experience that is unleashed upon them.

Phenomena are key with clients whose minds lean towards analysis. As they are frequently in trance, they may not experience it in the same way that others do. Further, they may not be aware of it when they do.

So, these may be the clients who tend to say things like, "I did not feel as if I was in hypnosis." However, that is less of an issue when you have just taken them on an experiential journey that involved their hand floating into the air and their foot being stuck to the floor!

When such an approach to inductions is undertaken effectively, there is no longer any need to fear the so-called analytical client. And confusion as a battle-of-the-wits becomes a thing of the past.

Rather than opposing someone's analytical mind, we can use the induction to lead them through an experiential process where they learn just how powerful their mind is. We can therefore begin to look forward to working with such clients, recognising that they bring great strengths to the hypnotic encounter. Instead of battling and belittling such powerful minds, let's welcome them and learn with them.

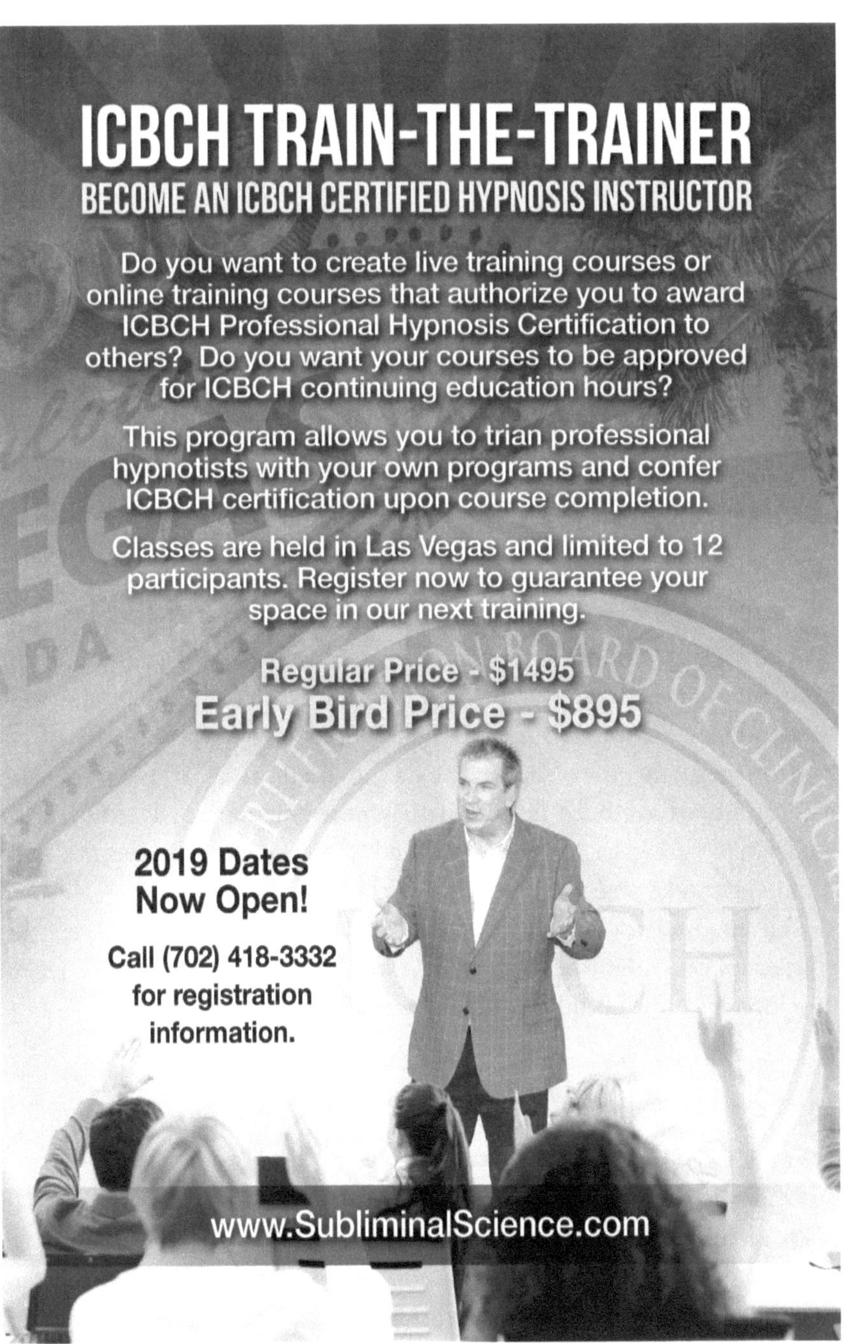

www.SubliminalScience.com

HYPNOSIS: EVIDENCE BASED TREATMENT FOR POSTTRAUMATIC STRESS DISORDER (PTSD)

RICHARD D. DAMA, LPC

EVEN IF YOU are not a clinician, if you have paid any attention to the news in the last decade or so, you are sure to have heard of the term Post-traumatic Stress Disorder (PTSD). Since our involvement in Iraq, Afghanistan and the Middle East, the medical and mental health communities have been dealing with a near epidemic of PTSD, all the while bemoaning the lack of qualified professionals to treat the large numbers of men and women seeking help.

Given the increased attention and resources devoted to this condition, one might be tempted to think that PTSD is a new or recent development, but nothing could be farther from the truth.

What is PTSD

Many articles and dissertations have been written about PTSD in history. One of the most concise outlines can be found at www.myptsd.com [1] with an account from 1000 BC wherein an Egyptian combat veteran named Hori wrote about the feelings he experienced before going into battle: "You determine to go forward…

Shuddering seizes you, the hair on your head stands on end, your soul lies in your hand."

Herodotus wrote of the Spartan commander Leonidas, who at the battle of Thermopylae in 480 BC dismissed men from his famous '300' because he recognized they were psychologically spent from previous battles. "They had no heart for the fight and were unwilling to take their share of the danger."[2]

As we can see, PTSD has been with us for thousands of years and at various times it was referred to by different names:

- During the US Civil War PTSD symptoms were described as "soldier's heart" or "exhaustion"
- During WWI, PTSD symptoms were known as "shell shock."
- During WWII, those with PTSD symptoms were said to have "battle fatigue," "combat fatigue" or "gross stress reaction."
- And in 1952, the APA listed what we now know as PTSD as "stress response syndrome." [3]

Unfortunately, it was not until the height of the Viet Nam War that clinicians realized that these symptom clusters were not just weakness or cowardice, but a legitimate medical/psychological diagnosis. Even then it was referred to as "Post-Vietnam Syndrome." [4]

It was not until 1980 that the American Psychiatric Association (APA) added PTSD to the third edition of the Diagnostic and Statistical Manual of Mental Disorders. [5] Even then, it was included primarily on anecdotal evidence and a paper written by Sarah Haley. It was not until work had begun on the DSM-IV that anyone bothered to conduct scientific field trials. [6]

As with any new idea, the DSM-III inclusion was a cause for fierce controversy. One of the biggest points of contention was that the diagnostic criteria required the catastrophic stressor be outside the range of usual human experience. Authors of the original PTSD diagnosis assumed traumas such as war, torture, rape, natural disasters such as earthquakes, and volcanoes, and human-made disasters such as factory explosions, airplane crashes, and automobile accidents. [6]

In the later DSM-IV (1994) and the DSM-IV-TR (2000) diagnostic criteria for PTSD included a history of exposure to a traumatic event and symptoms from each of three symptom clusters: intrusive recollections, avoidant/numbing symptoms, and hyper-arousal symptoms. A fifth criterion concerned duration of symptoms; and, a sixth criterion stipulated that PTSD symptoms must cause significant distress or functional impairment. [6]

The release of the DSM-5 in 2013) made a number of evidence-based revisions to PTSD diagnostic criteria. Most notably PTSD is no longer categorized as an Anxiety Disorder, but rather classified in a new category, Trauma- and Stressor-Related Disorders, in which the onset of every disorder has been preceded by exposure to a traumatic or otherwise adverse environmental event and the symptoms must have had their onset or been significantly exacerbated after exposure to the traumatic event. [5]

Prevalence of PTSD

About 3.6% of adult Americans -- about 5.2 million people -- suffer from PTSD during the course of a year, and an estimated 7.8 million Americans will experience PTSD at some point in their lives. PTSD can develop at any age, including childhood. Women are more likely to develop PTSD than are men. This may be due to the fact that women are more likely to be victims of domestic violence, abuse, and rape. [6]

What is Hypnosis?

Very much like PTSD, hypnosis has had a very long and storied history. When asked, most practitioners will probably cite the 18th century physician, Franz Mesmer and his theory of 'Animal Magnetism" as one of the earliest examples of therapeutic hypnosis...and they would be wrong. In fact they would be wrong by about 3300 years.

Records indicate that circa 2000 BCE the Egyptian priest Imhotep. (I-em-HO-tep, 'He comes in peace,') established healing sanctuaries called "Sleep or Dream Temples," where people were put into a trance like sleep; priests and priestesses then interpreted the person's dreams to gain knowledge about and find a cure for the illnesses. Even today, shrine sleep can be found in some parts of the Middle East and Africa. [7]

Other great hypnosis luminaries through the ages include Scottish surgeon James Braid, Sigmund Freud, and most recently Dave Elman and Milton Erickson.

Unfortunately, even with this well documented history and scientific basis, most people have a highly distorted idea as to what hypnosis entails. Television and movies typically depict the hypnotist as a greasy old man in a ratty office when a young and beautiful client comes in and the hypnotist says, "Look deep into my eyes" and the next thing you know the client is running down the street naked. Nothing could be farther from the truth. I actually have a very nice office.

Alright already, what exactly is hypnosis? Well the truth is that you will probably get as many answers to that question as people you ask.

Putting aside the ongoing State/Non-state debate, based on the history and evidence it is clear that the phenomenon of hypnosis exists and is being used, quite successfully as we will see, to treat a host of psychological and physical ailments.

For the purposes of brevity and clarity, I suggest an unofficial, but highly workable definition of:

Hypnosis, especially hypnotherapy, is an induced state of mind where the client is receptive to suggestions.

Hypnotic Phenomena

The point of hypnotherapy is to create change in our clients quickly and permanently using hypnotic phenomena. The most common hypnotic phenomena include:

- **Catalepsy** – This is when there is a locking of the muscles, and reduction of psychomotor activity resulting in the ability for the subject to maintain a specific posture of position for a long period of time without the sense of fatigue. Examples of this is making the arm stiff and rigid like an iron bar....

- **Time Distortion** – As indicated by its name, the client can experience expansion or dilation of their perception of time. This phenomenon can be spontaneous or suggested by the therapist.
- **Dissociation** – It is the dissociation of the subconscious from conscious mind, suspending the analytical thought processes.
- **Amnesia** – Inability to remember events of the past.
- **Hallucinations** – These can be both positive and negative in nature. A negative hallucination is having the subject not see; hear smell, etc., something that is actually there. A positive hallucination is the subject experiencing environmental stimuli that are not really there.
- **Post Hypnotic Suggestion** – I this is self-explanatory.
- **Analgesia** – This is the dulling in the awareness of pain, this is slightly different to anesthesia, which results in the complete lack of pain awareness. An example of this is having numbness in body parts, allowing to be pricked by a needle with no feeling, there are extreme cases such as where Dave Elman used this technique during a heart transplant as the patient was allergic to medical anesthetic. [8]

Peer Reviewed Evidence of the Efficacy of Hypnosis for PTSD

Let us begin by agreeing hypnosis works and is recognized as an effective treatment modality for many issues. In fact a quick Internet search of "Peer reviewed evidence of the effectiveness of hypnosis" will yield at least 235,000 results. [9] So the efficacy of hypnosis is not at issue.

So too, a search of "Peer reviewed evidence of the effectiveness of hypnosis for PTSD" yields 303,000 results.[10] I believe we can agree that based on this evidence, the efficacy of hypnotherapy itself and in the treatment of PTSD is beyond contention.

With this in mind, it will obviously be impossible to cover every study and technique included in the results. Rather I will spend our time discussing the most recent results that indicate the commonalities across all these studies and even more importantly, the techniques and clinical interventions that show the most promise in the treatment of this disorder.

For those still not convinced by my evidence so far, I want to call attention to a meta-analysis published in 2016 in the International Journal of Clinical and Experimental Hypnosis which concluded:

A large effect in favor of hypnosis-based…treatment was found for the studies that reported the posttest results. Temporal stability of the effect remains strong, as reflected by the 4-week follow-up assessments also by long-term evaluations (e.g., 12 months). **Hypnosis appears to be effective in alleviating PTSD symptoms.** [11]

In her book *Effective Treatments for PTSD,* Dr. Edna Foa, cites two randomized, controlled clinical trials. The first study concluded that hypnosis significantly decreased intrusion and avoidance symptoms, and seemed to do it in fewer sessions than the comparison treatments; while the second study found that hypnosis plus cognitive-behavioral therapy (CBT) had a larger therapeutic effect for re-experiencing episodes than did CBT alone.

These studies concluded by indicating a three-phase treatment protocol:

- Stabilization
- Re-experiencing
- Adaptive skills. [12]

Similarly, a 2005 article in the Journal of Consulting and Clinical Psychology, describes a study in which 87 civilian trauma survivors were randomly assigned to 6 sessions of CBT, CBT combined with hypnosis (CBT-hypnosis), or supportive counseling (SC). The authors found that fewer participants in the CBT and CBT-hypnosis groups met criteria for posttraumatic stress disorder at post treatment and 6-month follow-up than those in the SC group. CBT-hypnosis resulted in greater reduction in re-experiencing symptoms at post treatment than CBT. [13]

An intervention that has gained a lot of attention in recent years is Ego-State Therapy (EST). Helen Watkins describes EST as:

Ego-state therapy is a psychodynamic approach in which techniques of group and family therapy are employed to resolve conflicts between various "ego states" that constitute a "family of self" within a single individual. [14]

The most recent and far-reaching study on this topic appeared in the American Journal of Clinical Hypnosis in 2013. In it a single 5-6 hour manualized abreactive ego state therapy session was subjected to two placebo-controlled investigations that met evidence-based criteria. The researchers concluded that EST is a highly effective and durable treatment for posttraumatic stress disorder. [15]

Some colleagues may take exception with the following, but I firmly believe that evidence is not the sole purview of the academic journals, but also resides in the experiences of professional practitioners. In my 45 years of hypnosis experience, I have worked with countless PTSD clients and I know what has worked for me and them and my experience is exactly in line with the studies previously cited as well as Foa's three phase protocol of 1. Stabilization; 2. Re-experiencing; and 3. Helping the client develop adaptive skills.

The important thing to remember in this approach is that the client is going to have to undergo re-experiencing the traumatic experience(s), which more often than not results in abreactions. This is why it is absolutely critical that if you are working with a PTSD survivor, you are adequately trained, have received adequate supervision and are practicing within the scope of your competency. Ordinarily I would say that it is difficult to cause damage with hypnosis, but in this case, if you do not know what you are doing, you not only can exacerbate your client's condition, but probably will. So please practice responsibly.

References:

1. *History of post-traumatic stress disorder.* (2005). Retrieved

from: https://www.myptsd.com/history-of-post-traumatic-stress-disorder-ptsd/91/

2. *Gabriel, R., (1987). No More Heroes: Madness and Psychiatry In War.* New York, New York: McMillan.

3. *Psychiatric Disorders and Mental Health Issues.* (2014). Retrieved from: http://psychiatric-disorders.com/post-traumatic-stress-disorder/ptsd-history/

4. American Psychiatric Association. (1980). Diagnostic and statistical manual of mental disorders, (3rd ed.). Washington, DC: Author.

5. WebMd. (2016). *Posttraumatic stress disorder.* Retrieved from: https://www.webmd.com/mental-health/post-traumatic-stress-disorder#2

6. Friedman, M. (2016). *A brief history of the PTSD diagnosis. Washington, DC: US Department of Veterans Affairs.* Retrieved from: https://www.ptsd.va.gov/professional/PTSD-overview/ptsd-overview.asp

7. Reeves, D. (2017). *Hypnosis in ancient civilizations.* The Cuyamungue Institute. Santa Fe, NM. Retrieved from: http://www.cuyamungueinstitute.com/articles-and-news/hypnosis-in-ancient-civilizations/

8. Peterson, D. (2010). *Getting you rigid…hypnotic phenomena explained.* Recovered from: http://www.subliminalhacking.net/2010/10/29/getting-you-rigid-hypnotic-phenomena-explained/

9. Google search. (2018). *Peer reviewed evidence of the effectiveness of hypnosis.*

10. Google search. (2018). *Peer reviewed evidence of the effectiveness of hypnosis for PTSD.*

11. Ioan-Cuza, A., Rotaru, T., & Rusu, A. (2016). A meta-analysis for the efficacy of hypnotherapy in alleviating PTSD. Intl. Journal of Clinical and Experimental Hypnosis, 64(1): 116–136.

12. Foa, E. (2009). *Effective treatments for PTSD, (2nd ed.).* New York, NY: Guilford Press.

13. Bryant, R., Guthrie, R., Moulds, M., & Nixon, R. (2005).

The additive benefit of hypnosis and cognitive-behavioral therapy in treating acute stress disorder. Journal of Consulting and Clinical Psychology, 73(2), 334-340. Retrieved from: http://psycnet.apa.org/record/2005-02854-017.

14. Watkins, H. (1993). *Ego-state therapy: an overview.* American Journal of Clinical Hypnosis, 35(4), 232-240.

15. Barabasz A. (2013). *Evidence based abreactive ego state therapy for PTSD.* American Journal of Clinical Hypnosis, 56(1), 54-65.

A CLINICAL HYPNOTIST IN STAGE HYPNOTIST'S CLOTHING…

MICHAEL DESCHALIT

"I'M one of those guys. I'm a stage Hypnotist. You know, the guys that do the shows and get people to do funny stuff on stage." That is the statement that I make to ALL of my clinical clients during the initial consultation. I go on by stating that I tell them this in fairness in case they research me and discover this on their own. You see, I don't want any of my clinical work affected by clients who might have jaded or biased thoughts about what I'm going to "make them do" when they are in hypnosis. So, there's the rub… This is the age-old debate about stage hypnosis within most clinical hypnosis circles. There is still a huge misconception as to whether stage hypnosis hurts the clinical industry. I get it and totally understand that perception, or misconception. I really do get it not only being a practitioner and trainer of both stage and clinical hypnosis and having seen thousands of clients and even more thousands of volunteers that have been on my stage. I know first hand what some people think of hypnosis. Yes, I know that there are some stage hypnotists that perform shows that are beyond the Vegas Adult Hypnosis shows and get their volunteers to do things that are not only inappropriate but borderline dangerous. I also know that all it takes is one clinical hypnotist to do something inappropriate or out of the scope of their professional ability [dangerous] to make the whole profession look bad. So rather than turn this into a debate, the same age-old debate, let's explore how stage hypnosis can benefit clinical hypnosis and how clinical hypnotists can learn a thing or two that will not only enhance their abilities as a clinical hypnotist, but will also help their clients experience even greater results.

As a stage hypnotist, I am literally in front of audiences of anywhere from 100 to 2500 for every show. I can't think of a better platform from where to speak about hypnosis. Built into the scripting of my show I have my pre-talk which describes to the audience and potential volunteers what hypnosis is, is not, how it works, what they can expect to experience, and… here's the best part… the many uses of hypnosis. This is my time to educate the audience about what we as hypnotists use hypnosis for and what the audience has available to them as a remedy to a myriad of "things" that stop them from achieving their true potential in life. I will mention that hypnosis is great for smoking cessation, weight management, stress control, eliminating fears and bad habits, pain management for dentistry, childbirth and other medical issues, as well as enhancement and peak performance programs for athletes and business professionals. After all, I have a captive audience, why not mention all of that?

Another mention from the stage that I found helpful to the clinical hypnosis profession is to promote the local hypnotists. Since I travel across the country performing shows at schools, colleges, churches, fairs and festivals, corporate functions, and private events; I don't often spend too much time in one place. So, seeing now that I have done a great job of explaining the many uses of hypnosis and I have the audience interested in using hypnosis for whatever reason, I must do an equally good job at educating them on where they can go for hypnosis services. My solution to that is simple… I promote the local hypnotists and direct the audience to support their local businesses. The very first thing I do when I get to the town where I am going to perform my show is check into my hotel room. The second thing I do, religiously, is to look in the phone book (yes, they still put them in hotel rooms) to see who the local hypnotists are. If I'm lucky enough to know them it's easy. I call them up, invite them to dinner and my show where I will do a "shout out" during my show to plug them and their business. If I do not know them,

I will call them up, invite them to dinner and my show where I will give them a "shout out" to promote them and their business. Yes, I really do that. I look at it this way, it's my way of giving back to the profession, and as a good friend and fellow hypnotist, Jason Linett, says "If one of us is successful, then we are all successful".

Something else I do, and other stage hypnotists are known for doing, is to sell hypnosis products at the end of our shows. Of course, this is a lucrative source for addition streams of income, since it's like having hundreds of people visit the products page of your clinical website at the same time. But the bigger picture is that it's the fastest way of getting more hypnosis products into the hands of the public. If you're good at math, you'll see past the dollars earned and realize that it's that fastest way to get people who have never been exposed to hypnosis to try it out. It is simple math you see; the more people that try hypnosis, the more people that realize it has some benefits, value, and it works. Again, everybody wins here because then they might just want to go to their local hypnotist, now that they have been exposed to it, and have a greater level of comfort and understanding. As opposed to those not wanting to go to a hypnotist because they are afraid of what's going to happen and stage hypnosis being their only choice to try it out.

Now I want to switch gears here a little to focus more on the clinical side. Confidence is essential for any hypnotist, especially a stage hypnotist. Even so, it is necessary for a clinical hypnotist to exude a certain level of confidence, as your client picks up on that, and could even lead to their level of success. As a stage hypnotist and having to manage a dozen or so volunteers on stage at the same time can be overwhelming at first, but with practice it becomes second nature. It's that level of confidence that a stage hypnotist can bring into a clinical setting that helps to convince the client right from the initial consultation all the way through the final session that hypnosis is going to work.

Because stage hypnotists primarily use more authoritarian suggestions and approach, and clinical hypnotists are more permissive in their language; as a stage hypnotist, I have an advantage of "commanding" more attention with certain clients for certain issues by using my authoritarian style. This doesn't work for everything and every client, but it's a great tool to have in your clinical tool belt rather than only using a permissive approach, which in some cases isn't enough to motivate the clients subconscious to make the shift towards change. During my 16 years in practice as a clinical hypnotist, I have had hundreds of clients come to me BECAUSE I am a stage hypnotist. They have even gone on to say that they know that if I can "make" a dozen people on stage do "things", that I can "make" them quit smoking, or whatever else they have come to see me for. Of course I will make sure that I educate them to understand that I really don't "make" them do anything, in either setting.

In summary, I am a clinical hypnotist in stage hypnosis clothing and have learned that both have a place in this world. Both types of hypnotists can learn from each other on how to educate people on the benefits and uses of hypnosis, but most importantly, both can not only offer help, but deliver value to people. That, after all, is why I am a hypnotist, both stage and clinical.

IS THIS WHY HYPNOTHERAPY REALLY WORKS?

JOHN PHILIP MACHNIAK, LLPC

WHAT IS HYPNOSIS? What is the best way to hypnotize? Why do hypnotherapists have their own "pet" theories and methods? Is there one best way to achieve results? Questions…questions… What exactly *are* the answers? Is there any way to explain why there are hundreds of ways to hypnotize with hundreds of positive results? They cannot all be right or wrong.

Or could they?

Sorting it all out…

Arguing with another hypnotherapist about hypnotism and hypnotic techniques is frequently like discussing religion or politics with a "true believer" – NO ONE ever wins that one, because one side is convinced that it has "the answer" – the ONLY answer. But, what can account for the fact that hundreds of hypnotherapists use hundreds of different techniques yet all these hypnotists – and their techniques – can be equally effective under the right circumstances?

What can we learn from reflecting on that fact?

Plenty...

The work of psychologist David P. Fourie might be able to shed some light on this phenomenon. Fourie postulated what he called an "ecosystemic perspective on hypnosis" (Fourie, 1995). His work can be invaluable to hypnotherapists who are interested in trying to understand why diametrically opposed hypnotic theories and techniques can all equally produce positive outcomes under the right circumstances.

What is an Ecosystemic Perspective on Hypnosis?

The ecosystemic perspective posits a few ideas:

1. "*Hypnosis is a concept, not an entity*" (Fourie, 1995, p. 303). The concept of "hypnosis" is based upon the meaning that is given to occurring behaviors. These behaviors are labeled as "hypnotic" and given specific meaning as being "hypnotic."
2. "*Behavior gets mutually qualified as 'hypnotic'*" (Fourie, 1995, p. 303). Behavior that occurs in a situation that is defined as "hypnotic" is defined as such based on the context in which the behavior is taking place. It is identified as "hypnotic" by mutual consensus.
3. "*Hypnosis is not caused*" (Fourie, 1995, p. 303). Hypnosis, in Fourie's thinking, is based upon the attribution of meaning. Therefore, it can have no "cause."
4. "*Hypnosis is the definition of a constructed reality*" (Fourie, 1995, p. 303). Fourie takes the constructionist point of view. The concept of "hypnotherapy," he suggests, is based upon agreement between the parties involved in the process. The parties involved construct and mutually agree that what is taking place is "hypnotherapy."
5. "*The hypnotic reality exists in narrative*" (Fourie, 1995, p. 304). In other words, the "hypnotic reality" "is communicated meaning" (Fourie, 1995, p. 304).

Hypnotic Meaning and Hypnotic Rituals

The meaning that is attributed to hypnosis can include the beliefs that hypnosis is very powerful, threatening, ineffective or something else. Fourie points out that "clients and families often attribute mystical powers to hypnosis" (Fourie, 1995, p. 305). The view that hypnosis can be "powerful," for example, can enhance the efficaciousness of hypnosis in a therapeutic setting. The hypnotherapist can use a client's belief that hypnosis is "powerful" to help the client to achieve a better outcome by providing what Fourie refers to as "an expected ritual to which change can be ascribed" (Fourie, 1995, p. 305).

An important message that Fourie communicates is that hypnosis can be a powerful tool if the parties involved, including the hypnotherapist, attribute life-enhancing and life-changing meaning to the process. Fourie affirms that "The 'power' of hypnosis is the 'power' attributed to it by the client or family" (Fourie, 1995, p. 313).

A Fascinating Case Study

Fourie provided a good illustration of the social construction of hypnotherapy in a study that he conducted (2011).

Fourie maintained that a widely accepted view of hypnosis is that hypnotic suggestion somehow penetrates the unconscious mind (Fourie, 2011, p. 156). Fourie contended that this view is an attribution about hypnotherapy (Fourie, 2011, p. 158). To illustrate this contention, Fourie devised an experiment. The experiment involved a 30-year-old man who was suffering from anxiety and insomnia (Fourie, 2011, p 159). The client wanted to receive hypnotic suggestions that would influence his unconscious mind and provide him with some relief (Fourie, 2011, p. 159). The client believed, according to Fourie, the "currently popular view" that that is how hypnotic suggestions work (Fourie, 2011, p. 159).

The client was informed that he would not be aware of the suggestions that were being given to his subconscious mind because the suggestions "were meant for his unconscious mind." (Fourie, 2011, p. 160). Hypnosis was induced, but the suggestions that were agreed upon by the hypnotherapist and the client were *not* given to the client during hypnotherapy (Fourie, 2011, p. 160). The client, though, reported a positive outcome (Fourie, 2011, p 161).

What accounted for the positive outcome? Fourie contended that the process worked for the same reason that successful psychotherapy works – "a socially constructed and believable cognitive explanation or reframing of the origin of the problem followed by action consensually deemed appropriate to this explanation" (Fourie, 2011, p. 161). The belief of the client and the meaning that the client attributes to the therapeutic process, according to Fourie, is a key factor in how successful the outcome will be (Fourie, 2011, p. 162).

Takeaway Lessons to be Learned…

Hypnotherapists can learn a few things from Fourie's research that can help them to become more effective:

"I Do *This*, You Do *That*."

Hypnotherapy is a mutually agreed upon construction. In effect, "I," the hypnotherapist, will "do" something. "You," the client, will "do" something in response to what "I" do. If there is agreement on the part of the hypnotherapist and the client that the verbal and nonverbal suggestions have meaning and will be effective, most likely they will be. It is important for the hypnotherapist to be aware that there needs to be agreement by all parties involved vis-a-vis what is expected to happen during hypnotherapy. The expectation that "something constructive is going to happen" must be communicated to the client both verbally and nonverbally. Much of this communication, of course, can and should take place during the pre-talk. The realization that hypnotherapy is a mutually agreed upon construction has important practical applications for the reflective hypnotherapist to consider.

It's All Made Up…And Why That Matters

Since the hypnotherapeutic process is a "constructed reality," it is reasonable to conclude that there is not necessarily one specific induction, deepener or method of formulating and delivering suggestions that is necessarily better than another. That is good news. It means that the thoughtful hypnotherapist can stop spending an inordinate amount of time learning "just one more technique" or attending "just one more seminar" or reading "just one more book." Of course, this does not mean that skill development is not a good or necessary thing. It does mean, though, that the reflective therapist can consider spending more productive time thinking about the way that clients conceptualize the process of hypnotherapy. With this knowledge, the reflective therapist can then devise and implement practical strategies to capitalize on their new-found knowledge.

Knowing that the hypnotherapeutic process is a constructed reality also means realizing that negative outcomes in the past might not necessarily have been the result of something that either the hypnotherapist or the client did "wrong." Perhaps negative outcomes are the result of the absence of a mutually agreed upon reality. Since Fourie's theories suggest that it matters that the hypnotherapist and client have a consensus that what is happening will lead to positive outcomes, the wise hypnotherapist who has experienced negative outcomes might consider giving their attention to how they can help to structure and create consensus with future clients.

Where to Go to from Here…

A good way to learn about the social constructionist view of hypnotherapy is to study the "masters" of the past. When you research the masters of the past, remember that hypnotherapy was frequently written about under different names, such as "suggestion," "autosuggestion," "psychotherapy," "the occult," "mesmerism," "influence" and "magnetism." Look at what the masters did that appeared to work for them. Study their works from the point of view of Fourie's research, knowing that the masters of the past constructed a reality and context for hypnotherapy that was proper for their time, culture and individual personalities. Study, especially, *why* it appears that they approached hypnotherapy as they did. What did they do? How did they do it? Why did they do it? Is there a common theme that you notice in the work of the successful and famous hypnotists that you study? Learn from them and try to successfully apply what you learn to contemporary times.

Who knows? Maybe your discoveries will help you to become a modern-day Anton Mesmer or James Braid.

References

Fourie, D. P. (1995, April). Attribution of meaning: An ecosystemic perspective on hypnotherapy. *American Journal of Hypnotherapy, 36*(4), 300-315.

Fourie, D.P. (2011). Social constructionism and the role of the unconscious in hypnotic responding: A single case experiment. *Behavior Change, 28*(3), 156-163.

USING HYPNOSIS TO IMPROVE SURGICAL OUTCOMES

MATT DEWILD RN, LMT, CPH, CHI

WITH OVER 48 Million surgical procedures performed in the U.S. annually[1], and complications from those surgeries rising as high as 30%[2] in some cases, with mortality rates potentially as high as 20%[3], additional methods to reduce post-operative complications are needed to reduce these numbers.

Patients, physicians, and the public as a whole have a vested interest in reducing complications from surgical procedures. Not only from a patient outcome perspective, but also from a financial aspect as well. One study looked at the costs associated with surgical complication found that cases with surgical complications cost third party payors and hospitals 119% more than those without[4]. Surgical complications more than doubling the cost associated with a particular procedure.

Hypnosis is one such option that can help improve surgical outcomes. From reducing post-operative pain, and subsequent pain medication use, to alleviating the stress and anxiety associated with the procedure itself, to improved wound healing, hypnosis has been researched and found to be beneficial in many key areas to can drastically improve surgical outcomes.

Key applications of hypnosis that can help improve surgical outcomes:

- **Reduce fear and anxiety prior to, and after a procedure** – Hypnosis has been utilized effectively for removing or reducing fears and phobias for hundreds of years. Fear and subsequent anxieties related to procedures result in an abnormally high stress response which can create increased inflammation, and a decrease in immune system function. A weakened immune system following a surgical procedure certainly increases the risk of infection and can delay wound healing. By decreasing fear and anxiety, there is less tension, which can result in better blood flow and oxygenation of the tissues. This reduces pain, speeds healing, and reduces infections.
- **Pain Management** – Post operative pain is big concern for patients. The conventional methods of pain management following a surgical procedure is achieved through pain medications. Often involving the use of opioid (narcotic) pain medication. These medications carry risks of their own including digestive problems, respiratory depression, and addiction. Having a mechanism to reduce the need for and usage of these medications can lead to better outcomes overall. Hypnosis for pain management is effective tool that can aid in the comfort of the patient and reduce complications that increased usage of pain medication can create.
- **Improved patient compliance** – Often times following a surgical procedure, patients need to perform certain tasks such as incentive spirometry or physical therapy to optimize outcomes. Pain, anxiety, and emotions can present barriers to the full and active participation in these activities. Hypnosis can serve to help remove these barriers and increase motivation for patients to participate in activities that will bring about better healing, better function, and better outcomes.

The theory sounds good, but does it really work?

There is considerable evidence in the research to support adding hypnosis in surgical cases for reducing pain and anxiety, to speed healing, and reducing overall complications.

Take for example, the study at Massachusetts General Hospital looking at adding hypnosis to the treatment of ankle fractures[5].

"Results showed trends toward faster healing for the hypnosis group through week 9 following injury. Objective radiographic outcome data revealed a notable difference in fracture edge healing at 6 weeks. Orthopedic assessments showing trends toward better healing for hypnosis subjects through week 9 included improved ankle mobility; greater functional ability to descend stairs; lower use of analgesics in weeks 1, 3, and 9; and trends toward lower self-reported pain through 6 weeks.[5] "

While this study looked at non-surgical ankle fracture management, the results of decreased pain and accelerated healing were certainly noted and could be extrapolated to surgical interventions as well.

Another study looked at wound healing following surgery using hypnosis combined with standard wound care compared to standard wound care measures alone. The results are very clear.

"The primary outcome data of interest were objective, observational measures of incision healing made at 1,7 weeks postoperatively by medical staff blind to the participants' group assignments. Data included clinical exams and digitized photographs that were scored using a wound assessment inventory (WAI). Secondary outcome measures included the participants' subjectively rated pain, perceived incision healing (VAS Scales), and baseline and post-surgical functional health status (SF-36).

Analysis of variance showed the hypnosis group's objectively observed wound healing to be significantly greater than the other two groups', $p <$ .001, through 7 postoperative weeks; standard care controls showed the smallest degree of healing. In addition, at both the 1 and 7 week post-surgical observation intervals, one-way analyses showed the hypnosis group to be significantly more healed than the usual care controls, $p <0.02$. The mean scores of the subjective assessments of postoperative pain, incision healing and functional recovery trended similarly.[6] "

A look at accelerated wound healing in burn patients specifically through hypnotic vasodilation. Independently evaluated by medical and nursing staff who where not aware of which side of the body had the added hypnosis treatment.

"This study was designed to assess the efficacy of hypnotically induced vasodilation in the healing of burn wounds. Patients were selected on the basis of having symmetrical or bilaterally equivalent burns on some portion of their right and left sides. Since one side only of the body was treated by hypnotically induced vasodilation, the patient served as his own experimental control. In this single blind study, the hypnotist and patient knew the side selected for treatment, the evaluating surgeon and nursing staff did not. Four of the five patients demonstrated clearly accelerated healing on the treated side, the fifth patient had rapid healing to both sides. It is concluded that hypnosis facilitated dramatic enhancement of burn wound healing.[7]"

This study looked at using hypnosis to decrease side effects of breast surgery such as anesthesia and analgesia usage as well as post-operative nausea, fatigue, discomfort, and emotional upset. This was done with a brief 15-minute presurgical hypnosis session.

"Patients in the hypnosis group required less propofol (means = 64.01 versus 96.64 µg; difference = 32.63; 95% confidence interval [CI] = 3.95 to 61.30) and lidocaine (means = 24.23 versus 31.09 mL; difference = 6.86; 95% CI = 3.05 to 10.68) than patients in the control group. Patients in the hypnosis group also reported less pain intensity (means = 22.43 versus 47.83; difference = 25.40; 95% CI = 17.56 to 33.25), pain unpleasantness (means = 21.19 versus 39.05; difference = 17.86; 95% CI = 9.92 to 25.80), nausea (means = 6.57 versus 25.49; difference = 18.92; 95% CI = 12.98 to 24.87), fatigue (means = 29.47 versus 54.20; difference = 24.73; 95% CI = 16.64 to 32.83), discomfort (means = 23.01 versus 43.20; difference = 20.19; 95% CI = 12.36 to 28.02), and emotional upset (means = 8.67 versus 33.46; difference = 24.79; 95% CI = 18.56 to 31.03). No statistically significant differences were seen in the use of fentanyl, midazolam, or recovery room analgesics. Institutional costs for surgical breast cancer procedures were $8561 per patient at Mount Sinai School of Medicine. Patients in the hypnosis group cost the institution $772.71 less per patient than those in the control group (95% CI = 75.10 to 1469.89), mainly due to reduced surgical time.

Hypnosis was superior to attention control regarding propofol and lidocaine use; pain, nausea, fatigue, discomfort, and emotional upset at discharge; and institutional cost. Overall, the present data support the use of hypnosis with breast cancer surgery patients.[8]"

This study shows a significant improvement over multiple criteria in the hypnosis group and demonstrated a financial savings in this group as well.

A look at using hypnosis with orthopedic hand surgery to improve post-operative outcomes.

"Orthopedic hand-surgery patients experience severe pain postoperatively, yet they must engage in painful exercises and wound care shortly after surgery; poor patient involvement may result in loss of function and disfigurement. This study tested a hypnosis intervention designed to reduce pain perception, enhance postsurgical recovery, and facilitate rehabilitation. Using a quasi-experimental research design, 60 hand-surgery patients received either usual treatment or usual treatment plus hypnosis. After controlling for gender, race, and pretreatment scores, the hypnosis group showed significant decreases in measures of perceived pain intensity (PPI), perceived pain affect (PPA), and state anxiety. In addition, physician's ratings of progress were significantly higher for experimental subjects than for controls, and the experimental group had significantly fewer medical complications. These results suggest that a brief hypnosis intervention may reduce orthopedic hand-surgery patients' postsurgical PPI, PPA, and anxiety; decrease comorbidity; and enhance postsurgical recovery and rehabilitation.[10]"

The literature contains many examples of the efficacy of hypnosis for improving surgical outcomes and reducing post-operative complications. Adding hypnosis as an intervention for surgical cases is a simple and cost-effective means to achieve these results. This can have a profound impact for patients, physicians, surgery centers, 3rd party payors, and the public as a whole.

1. Hall,Margaret, Schwartzman,Alexander, Zhang,Jin, and Liu, Xiang (2017). Ambulatory Surgery Data From Hospitals and Ambulatory Surgery Centers: United States: 2010. *National Health Statistics Report Number 102 February 28 2017.* https://www.cdc.gov/nchs/data/nhsr/nhsr102.pdf
2. Healey,Mark; Shackford, Steven; Osler, Turner; et al

Rogers,Frederick; Burns, Elizabeth (2002) Arch Surg. 2002;137(5):611-618. doi:10.1001/archsurg.137.5.611 https://jamanetwork.com/journals/jamasurgery/fullarticle/212419

3. Freundlich, Maile, Sferra, Jewell, Kheterpal, Engoren (2018). Anesthesia & Analgesia. Complications Associated With Mortality in the National Surgical Quality Improvement Program Database. https://www.ncbi.nlm.nih.gov/pubmed/29324497

4. Healy, Mullard, Campbell, Dimick (2016). Hospital and Payer Costs Associated With Surgical Complications: JAMA Surg. 2016 Sep 1;151(9):823-30. doi: 10.1001/jamasurg.2016.0773. https://www.ncbi.nlm.nih.gov/pubmed/27168356

5. Ginandes C, Rosenthal DI (1999). "Using Hypnosis to Accelerate the Healing of Bone Fractures." Alternative Therapies in Health and Medicine. 5(2): 67-75.

6. Ginandes C, Brooks P, Sando W, Jones C, Aker J. (2002). "Can Medical Hypnosis Accelerate Post-Surgical Wound Healing? Results of a Clinical Trial." American Journal of Clinical Hypnosis. 45(4): 333-51.

7. Moore, Lawrence & Kaplan, Jerold (2011). Hypnotically Accelerated Burn Wound Healing. Pages 16-19 | Published online: 22 Sep 2011. https://www.tandfonline.com/doi/abs/10.1080/00029157.1983.10404132

8. Guy H. Montgomery Dana H. Bovbjerg Julie B. Schnur Daniel David Alisan Goldfarb Christina R. Weltz Clyde Schechter Joshua Graff-Zivin Kristin Tatrow Donald D. Price et al (2007). A Randomized Clinical Trial of a Brief Hypnosis Intervention to Control Side Effects in Breast Surgery Patients. JNCI: Journal of the National Cancer Institute, Volume 99, Issue 17, 5 September 2007, Pages 1304–1312, https://doi.org/10.1093/jnci/djm106

9. Magaly H. Mauer , Kent F. Burnett , Elizabeth Anne Ouellette , Gail H. Ironson & Herbert M. Dandes (1997).

Medical hypnosis and orthopedic hand surgery: Pain perception, postoperative recovery, and therapeutic comfort. International Journal of Clinical and Experimental Hypnosis Volume 47, 1999 - Issue 2 Pages 144-161 | Received 24 Dec 1997, Published online: 31 Jan 2008.
https://doi.org/10.1080/00207149908410027

I ALREADY DID

JEFFREY RICHARDS, CPH

WHERE'S the tipping point between having a system or process in place to ensure that you have remembered every detail necessary to have a great session, and running on auto-pilot to the point that it feels like you're just going through the motions?

I don't have the perfect answer to that...yet. But I have learned that it is usually better to error on the side of going with the system. Otherwise, you run the risk of having a great story to tell.

Several years ago I was working with a woman who wanted to lose a significant amount of weight (100+ lbs.) and she had come to the office for her first appointment. And, as she sat down in my guest chair, I said to her the same thing I say to everyone at the beginning of their session: "And please do whatever you need to do to your phone so it doesn't ring or vibrate while you're here."

I'm pretty proud of that sentence. I put a lot of thought into coming up with something I could say to any client, no matter what sort of phone they have or how familiar they are with it, and they would understand the desired result and could figure out on their own the easiest way to get there. Some people will put their phone on Do Not Disturb, others can turn their ringer volume all the way down, and the rest don't bother with the more fiddly settings on their phone and just turn the thing off. Their phone is no longer a potential distraction and they got to choose how to take care of it. Usually it's a win-win.

"I already did," was her response.

And that's a perfectly acceptable response to that request. She already did. Fine. But if you have a background in NLP, you know that it's not just the content of a communication but also its qualities (pitch, timbre, volume, etc.) that convey the complete message. And let there be no question, the complete message here was, "I already took care of my phone, and you're a cretinous troglodyte for assuming otherwise."

OK, fine, I can work with that, I thought. I like being friendly with my clients but that isn't always possible. And her response told me a lot about her (or, at least, her feelings about being told what to do with her phone) that I was able to use to establish enough rapport for us to begin the work.

A week went by and it was time for her next session. It had been an especially busy week and the details of her prior session weren't particularly fresh in my mind so, as I escorted her into the office, I just said what I say to everyone at the beginning of their session: "And please do whatever you need to do to your phone so it doesn't ring or vibrate while you're here."

"I already did." I am still a cretinous troglodyte and I suffer from a weak memory, probably the result of poor breeding and a lack of moral fiber. Fine. I'm not there to be her friend; I'm there to help her lose weight.

And this continued for another four weeks: "Please...your phone...ring...vibrate..." And I'm still a cretinous troglodyte but she's given up hope that I'll change and doesn't seem to care as much as time passes.

Until Session Six! In the program I was using at the time, Session Six was the game-changer. It was as if Sessions One through Five gradually tightened a spring and Session Six released it powerfully and all at once. All of the suggestions, stories, metaphors and linguistic jiggery-pokery came together in Session Six.

That's how it was supposed to work.

Because, you see, by my sixth week working with this client, I had gotten smart. I don't exactly believe in signs, but when the universe whaps you over the head with the same sign, five weeks in a row, you're a special kind of special of you don't at least entertain the possibility that there's something going on that you should be paying attention to.

By Session Six, I finally figured out that she "already did."

Except, of course, she hadn't.

And it wasn't just that her phone rang during her session. It couldn't be that simple. No, I was literally — and I would like to pause for a moment and state that I don't care what the folks at Webster's say; "figuratively" is not an acceptable definition of "literally" — taking the breath with which I was going to utter the words which were going to release that metaphorical "spring" and create an a-ha! moment that would be the unification of everything we'd done up to that point...

And you know those canvas tote purses? The kind that are just open at the top with no flap or clasp or any other device that might keep noise inside? Yep, she had one of those and her phone was in it. And she had placed the tote on the floor right next to the chair in which she sat.

So her phone rings in her purse, right next to her chair, with nothing between her ears and the noise except the open air, literally as I am taking the breath with which I am going to say the words that are going to change her life,

And I wish that were the worst of it.

It wasn't.

You see, it was her husband calling. And she had a custom ringtone set up for her husband.

And so...you know that song, "I'm Too Sexy" by Right Said Fred?

So, now, *every* time a client comes into my office, I say to them, "And please do whatever you need to do so that your phone doesn't ring or vibrate while you're here." Because it's good to be flexible in your response to any situation, but sometimes it makes more sense to do what you always do the way you've always done it to ensure that everything gets done.

I use this story as an opener when I'm talking to groups of young people, both to break the ice and to get the audience members to silence their phones. Feel free to use this story yourself; attribute it to me and it becomes a great use of "quotes" from the NLP toolbox so the message is softened a little and it works even better.

And when you tell this story, make absolutely sure that your phone is silenced before you start. Because having your phone ring after you've told this story makes you look like an even more special kind of special. Or, at the very least, it gives you a good story to tell.

C:O:A:C:H TRAINING

Castorian & Overdurfian Advanced Conversational Hypnocoaching.
Premiere HypnoTherapy, NLP, HNLP & Coaching.
For beginners & professionals.

#1 - ZOETERMEER, HOLLAND, FEBRUARY 14TH-17TH 2019
#2 - LAS VEGAS, USA, MARCH 6TH-9TH 2019

CERTIFIED HYPNOSIS TRAINER

Our high level Train The Trainer. Get all the best presenter tools avaliable.
We will first develop you as a teacher, then focus on the content.
4 Future students, and the training is paid for.

SCOTTSDALE, USA, JUNE 6TH-14TH 2019

EVENTS & CONFERENCES

Theese conferences are our main conferences for 2019. We will be doing
talks & workshops at all of them. Please join us.

HPTI WINTER HYPNOSIS CONFERENCE, LAS VEGAS, FEBRUARY 25TH-27TH

HPTI MASTER CLASS, LAS VEGAS, FEBRUARY 28TH - MARCH 2ND

ACHE CONFERENCE, GLENDALE, CALIFORNIA, MARCH 22ND-24TH

HEARTLAND HYPNOSIS CONFERENCE, ST. LOUIS, APRIL 26TH-28TH

HYPNOTHOUGHTS LIVE, LAS VEGAS, AUGUST 16TH-18TH

WHY CHOOSE US?

1 We have guaranteed unique and modern content so you will be a leading force.

2 We have a triple international award winning trainer, featured TedX Speaker and international headliner as Master Trainers.

3 All students will get FREE access to VIP online content for even more resources.

4 We care for all students. Both beginners and professionals will learn new skills, guaranteed.

MORE EVENTS GO TO WWW.THEHYPNOACADEMY.COM FOR LATEST CHANGES AND NEW EVENTS

www.TheHypnoAcademy.com

HYPNOSIS WITH ATHLETES

JONI NEIDIGH, LMHC

FORTUNATELY, today's athletes recognize the need for mental preparation in order to

achieve their highest goals. Skills that allow athletes to handle pressure and adversity, concentrate, and develop a confident winning attitude are not only available, but essential.

I call these the "usual suspects" of athlete issues but these are only a few of the areas in which hypnosis can be useful.

When working with athletes who want to increase their confidence and create an inner dialogue that will help their performances, a great place to start is with an assessment of their mental toughness. Find out from the athlete what is going right and what is going wrong. Using collateral information from coaches and/or parents will enhance the process. Once all of the information is collected, it can be related to how the athlete is currently handling pressure and adversity, how well they are able to concentrate, and whether or not they have a winning attitude. By using this information, a personalized plan for changing the athletes' mental game can be developed. This is an ongoing work in progress which occurs over multiple sessions while techniques are being developed and applied. This process produces the best overall, consistent results.

So what does changing an athletes mental game actually mean? First, it involves daily reflection and practice. To be effective, athletes must train their mental game in the same way they train the physical and technical aspects of their sport. This is where the athlete begins to gather information at each practice and each competition. They become aware of what works and what hurts. This creates better awareness of what athletes have been doing, what habits they have created, and what they need to change. As their needs become clear, hypnosis is an excellent tool to help athletes begin to eliminate bad habits and replace them with what they need.

The athlete also begins setting specific goals and creating a plan of action for achieving those goals. Using hypnosis to visualize those goals is powerful, as it helps them clarify what they want while removing limitations. This also includes examining any current relaxation techniques they may be using so the hypnotherapist can assist the athlete in replacing and/or modifying them.

Another important role of the hypnotherapist is the development of a tool kit which will provide the athlete with a quick reference to help them at practice or in competitions. This tool kit can be developed through face-to face sessions, Skype, FaceTime, or other modalities of communication. The most useful tools include reducing anxiety when over-aroused at competitions, increasing energy when they are under-aroused, and recognizing and becoming aware of their own peak performance state.

Hypnotherapists are well-equipped to help athletes develop the laser focus needed in order to keep their self-talk and thoughts on what they want while learning to distract themselves from the things they cannot control at competitions. Developing an awareness of these potential distractions will assist the athlete in decreasing anticipatory anxiety and increasing confidence in handling situations. These tools include hypnosis and NLP techniques that will help the athlete to simply recognize and return their thoughts from hurtful to helpful self-talk, which will in turn facilitate a peak performance state that will increase their chances of success.

Hypnotherapy offers a way to introduce quick, effective, fun, and portable techniques to athletes who are most often already time poor because they are student-athletes or working professional athletes. This is an important concept to promote to coaches, parents, teams and athletes. The ability to use self-hypnosis audios, brief sessions, and portable techniques make it possible for the athlete to receive the tools they need to develop a winning mindset without adding more time and effort on their part. The athletes appreciate this element of the approach as it decreases stress and helps them to make any necessary adjustments for future competitions quickly and easily.

The role of the hypnotherapist can be multi-faceted. There are numerous issues that go beyond the above-mentioned "usual suspects." Some of those issues include assisting an athlete by preserving or regaining the joy of the sport, finding the right fit (coach, team, location, etc.), making important and stressful decisions related to college recruiting and transitioning from high school to college.

While hypnotherapists often do an excellent job of helping the athletes remove limits, they are often limiting themselves as professionals by not applying their talents to help with other less obvious issues. Hypnosis can be useful with coaches, parents, and teams in many ways. For example, team talks introducing an understanding of hypnosis and demonstrating techniques are not only exciting and motivating, but often result in multiple client referrals.

When athletes move up to the professional level there are even higher expectations as money factors in. College athletes may face scholarship loss if they underperform. Overthinking this issue and being consumed with anticipatory anxiety can often result in a self-fulfilling prophecy. Athletes at higher levels are required to participate in media interviews and may have negative reactions to media hype. Although the client ultimately leads the hypnotherapist to the issue they want to resolve, hypnotherapists' awareness and ability to identify other pressing issues is important in order to help the athlete achieve overall success.

The involvement of hypnotherapists in athletics is increasing. Programs are recognizing the need for quicker, more permanent, and more effective techniques to help increase athletic performance and the overall well-being of the student athletes or professionals.

Joni Neidigh is a licensed mental health counselor in the state of Florida, a certified clinical hypnotherapist and a trainer for ICBCH and HPTI. She specializes in athletic performance and works with athletes from age-groupers to Olympians and professionals. Joni is the author of AIM Gold Medal Mental Toughness Success Guide and has produced over 30 self-hypnosis audios to help with athletic performance.

STOP SMOKING SCRIPT – 24 HOURS AFTER THE LAST CIGARETTE

DR. RICHARD K. NONGARD

www.SubliminalScience.com

Pre-Talk

CONGRATULATIONS! It has been more than 24 hours since you have had your last cigarette and you can be proud of that accomplishment!

In this hypnosis session you will take your change to the next level and ratify the experience you have had with hypnosis to produce lasting change. The great news here, is that this change you have made is not a temporary change but one you can commit in this session to lasting change.

In your previous session you created what we call a hypnotic anchor. You touched the thumb and index finger together, as if making an OK sign, and pressed those fingers together. Go ahead, get comfortable in the chair where you are, and close your eyes… Touch that thumb and index finger together right now and hold that tension together for a moment.

And relax the fingers. and notice something, your breath is calm and your heartrate has slowed, and you have instantly brought about the state of calm that you created in our last session right here and right now, just by touching those fingers together. It feels good doesn't it?

Now open the eyes again. In the past day you easily went without smoking. The things that were in fact cues to light up, were probably just a passing thought for you. Amazing, isn't it? You can congratulate yourself for a job well done. I don't know if you used that anchor, and touched you thumb and index finger together, a lot or a little but over the next day or two, or even the next week or two, anytime you need to bring yourself back to a commitment to change and feel the positive energy of your hypnosis practice, you can touch those fingers together and revivify this resources state. And of course when you do, you will notice any cue or craving pass quickly, leaving you with a sense of freedom, and health, and success.

Let's take your success to the next level.

On the screen in front of you is a sentence. Read the sentence you see and count all of the F's (the letter F) that you see.

(5 second break to read)

Did you count them? Count them again if you want to.

How many F's did you count?

Did you count 3? Most people do.

Did you count 4? Some people find the extra F

But did you see 5? Or were you one of the few (show highlighted F image) who was able to find all 6 of the F's?

Most people count 3. What that tells us that even when something is right in front of us, our conscious awareness is often limited. Through the hypnotic suggestions in your previous session – and the hypnotic suggestions we are going to share in this session you are going to bring all of your resources for success into awareness.

You can think of it this way – when you were smoking you weren't even looking for an F.

But in our last hypnosis session you began looking for some solutions – and you found them At least three of them. We know this because you have not smoked for at least the past 24 hours and it feels great to be successful.

But now we are going to uncover the rest of your inner resources and make this change a forever change.

The first thing we are going to uncover is your ability to stay in the present moment – this is called mindfulness. By keeping your thought, your emotions, and the sensations you experience in the present moment you will avoid rumination, obsessive thoughts or tempting yourself with unhealthy choices.

Mindfulness is all about staying present, because no matter what else is going on in life, or what stressors or temptations exist, right now – in this moment- everything is actually OK. It was the great Master Oogway who put it this way, "Yesterday is history, tomorrow is a mystery, all we have is the present – and that is why it is a gift."

Anytime, in any area of life, you can bring your attention to the present and you will discover that it is a gift. It is a gift of calm, of comfort, of success, and even a gift of acceptance. You do not have to follow a thought to be anxious, or stressed, or of the sensation of withdrawal and project into the future any temptation to smoke. You can just remain in the present moment, and just breath, and discover mindfulness is a real solution – not only to smoking, but really in every area of life.

Go ahead, close your eyes down. Pay attention to your breath as you breathe right now. Bring all of your attention to your breath, almost like you are studying your breath. Pay attention to the nostrils as you breath in, and the feeling of air being drawn into your lungs. You do not have to breath in any special way, this is not yoga, so just breathe, and pay attention to the breath.

Notice that point in the lungs when the air turns around, kind of like an Olympic swimmer in a swimming pool, and the inhale becomes an exhale.

Good. You are paying attention to your breath, and each breath marks each moment.

Now, your mind will continue to think as you sit in this chair, you will have thoughts, you will have feelings and emotions and you will have physical sensations. Hypnosis – or mindfulness – is not about turning off these thoughts, feelings or sensations, but rather learning that when you have them you do not have to follow them – you can simply recognize them as a thought and use them as a cue or a reminder to return your thought to the breath. The breath is a focal point. It is where you are going to practice returning your attention. Do this not only right now, but in every area of life thorough each day, and you will discover it becomes second nature to stay in the moment.

Now, open the eyes. go ahead, open them again.

Mindfulness may or may not seem that important right now, but the value is in practicing bringing your attention from any temptation, distraction, or tension and back to the present moment. People who have anxiety find that by practicing mindfulness each day it becomes second nature, and that they feel less anxious and more happy.

One of the reasons we practice hypnosis and mindfulness is to help sort out what is a trick of the mind or distorted thinking. Former smokers sometimes pay attention to mind tricks, wondering if "just one would hurt them" or if even questing if they really wanted ot quit smoking – or as I like to call it – start breathing clean air.

Mind tricks can be powerful, we explored some in the last session.

Right now you are looking at the image of some shiny legs. How did they make that shine? When most people see these shiny legs for the first time, they are amazed by the glossiness and sheen they have.

That is of course, until it is revealed that the legs are not shiny at all – rather they have been painted with white lines and dots.

Once the paint is revealed, even when people want to see the shininess again, they usually can't.

That part of your mind that used to believe to believe that smoking was acceptable, has been replaced with the white paint of the last 24 hours. No matter how much that part of the mind that plays tricks on us might want to return to old ideas – you now know that smoking is not for you.

What is most important to you in this moment? Is it the new health you have? In just the first 24 hours of quitting smoking heart attack risk begins to decrease, nerve endings are restored to the sensations of taste and smell, and carbon monoxide levels have decreased, and your blood cells can once again bond with oxygen.

Or is it the money in your pocket? It felt pretty good to not buy more cigarettes yesterday. In fact, you might have even saved up enough to buy a half tank of gas with the savings you have had in just the past 24 hours.

I bet the people who love you are really happy you have made this change. And of course, if you are looking for love, you just expanded your dating pool by up to 70%.

It feels good to be in this moment. Take in a breath. Be here right now, fully present in this session and congratulate yourself – and even let yourself smile.

Oh year, the color red, did you notice it a bit brighter and sharper and crisper and clearer? It was a handy reminder wasn't it? It's funny how when something is suggested to us – that we will notice the color red – it becomes present everywhere – just as your success with this change has become very apparent to both others and yourself.

Are you ready to begin? To take hypnosis to the next level and ratify this change? Then let's begin!

Beginning of actual session – notice, there is no formal induction, the process/story is and of itself, induction.

Inspirational speaker Joel Osteen has said, "You have to come to your closed doors before you get to your open doors... What if you <u>knew</u> you had to go through 32 closed doors before you got to your open door? Well, then you'd come to closed door number eight and you'd think, 'Great, I got another one out of the way' and you would keep on going.

This is of course, exactly what you have done. You have probably gone through many doors to become a non-smoker. Attempts to quit smoking by cutting down, another door using your willpower to go cold turkey, another door to try medication and more doors that included promises, resolutions and still others doors along this journey. For many people – hypnosis seems to be popular as door 32 – the last door. And so, here you are now a non-smoker. You have arrived at your destination, the hard work is behind you and you have at least 24 hours of success behind you, and maybe even 32!

None of that was wasted time or energy, they were the doors you needed to go through to get to the last door, and discover where you are today. In fact, I bet there was a time when some of those doors led to your success for a day or two or even a couple of weeks or even a couple of years. The real question now is not actually can you quit? You have already proved that you can. The real question now is now that you have reached door 32, how do we go further than you have at any other point.

And so close your eyes.

Imagine now that you are standing in front of a closed door. You know you have to pass through this door to get to where you want to go, but when you knock, nobody answers. It is a closed door. But you have a key that will open the door, and so in your mind, imagine unlocking the closed door, opening it and walking through.

Imagine that this door leads to a large room filled with interesting art and furniture, and relaxing music that is playing. Go ahead, imagine taking a seat on the recliner and just enjoy the relaxing ambiance of this room. In this place and in this space, you have unlocked the first door of your new life and can just relax in this space.

This is of course, a perfect place to practice mindfulness – just being present. Your conscious mind obviously wants to know what lies on the other side of the next door, but right now practice what we learned before you closed your eyes, and be mindful. Study your breath, and be in this moment. What a perfect place to really practice. The mind does what minds do, it wonders and wanders, maybe even looking beyond the next door. And of course, all you have to do it see this as it is, a cue to be present in this room and return your attention to the breath.

In this time and this space, just be relaxed. Nowhere to go and nothing to do, letting yourself go deeper into this moment.

Ever number and every breath, a cue to stop chasing your thoughts and enjoy the moment

5

4

3

2

1

0

Perfect.

It feels pretty good to just be. No stress, no worries, letting go absolutely of any expectations.

Go ahead, open your eyes. Feels good doesn't it?

Another closed door. But this door requires no key, you have already unlocked it by mastering being present in the moment, by being mindful.

Imagine opening this door, go ahead, turn the knob, and entering a room filled with white light and healing and energy that empowers you. And close your eyes again….

Imagine what that the healing energy of this room literally clears your body from any damage smoking may have done and discover a renewed spirit of hope – knowing that you have done something wonderful for your body by becoming a non-smoker. Notice the next breath, an easier breath than the labored breaths you used to take just days ago. You body has begun healing in every way and this will continue every day and you are getting better and better with each breath and each passing moment.

Go ahead, open the next closed door. the door of identity – in the past you identified as a smoker. Looking for restaurants that permitted smoking, and avoiding place where you would be unable to smoke. Perhaps in the past you even collected the accoutrements of smoking, ash trays, lighters and even logo memorabilia, content to be a smoker. In your younger days smoking might have even been a way to identify with others, and to set yourself apart from those you did wish to identify with. It does seem immature to our logical mind at this point in our lives, but in our younger days the habit of smoking was probably ingrained with the identity of being a smoker. After all, cigarette ads used to show the independent woman, or the debonair man – and cigarette marketers have studies hypnosis – knowing these imprints, conscious or subconscious influenced our choices. In some ways, by opening this door you are actually de-hypnotizing yourself from the messages of the tobacco industry, some overt and some subliminal.

To help you a re-write these associations, I have embedded this experience with positive affirmations and "I am" statements that really do correspond to your current identity – one who rejects smoking and embraces wellness. One who is strong not because of an image but strong because of real change that has already taken place.

In fact, at this point, with 10% of the 32 closed doors open: Mindfulness, healing and identity it might even seem counter-intuitive to go deeper, and so imagine the next closed door is up a few steps, and when you open this closed door – which we shall call commitment you discover a pathway of closed doors, each taking you to a higher level of consciousness a higher level of awareness and a higher level of success

Number 5

Number 6

Number 7

pushing through each closed door and making your way forward – feeling motivated to succeed knowing that this time, you have pushed through so many closed doors to get to the next that as you push through door 8

and door 9

and door 10-11-12 and 13

that with each closed door opened, it gets easier and easier to move to the end.

What is it either know or unknown that has limited your prior success? Maybe it is something obvious to you, a situation, or a feeling or an personality characteristic that you have struggled with – or perhaps it is something unknown deep in your psyche and makeup – it doesn't really matter if it is easily identifiable or if it is something unidentifiable, as you push through the next closed door – illuminating your path you can leave it behind door number 14

moving forward past 15 and 16 and opening the door to number 17.

Of course, at this point you may still be paying attention to every work I say, following the process step by step, or you may be in deep trance, only paying attention to some of the words that I use, choosing to experience the process rather than listen to it, and either way is OK. People experience hypnosis in many different ways – and what is amazing to me is that they all seem to discover that it leads them to the last door – an open door that never closes – to lasting change.

You have made this change already – by experiencing our first session and ratifying it with this session.

I'll give you the next couple of minutes to imagine the next closed doors being opened, and discovering behind each closed door whatever is most important to you in creating lasting success. Maybe it will be hope, maybe it will be forgiveness, maybe it will be self-acceptance or even a recognition that by not smoking you are not alone, but rather, have been joined by perhaps millions of other people who have quit the same way....

During this time, you may hear embedded subliminal affirmations, or perhaps you will not, either way is fine, your higher consciousness is ready to accept the new possibilities and the infinite you. I will rejoin you on your journey through the last two doors.

SILENCE 90 seconds duration

You are almost there. To the 32nd door. You have pushed open every closed door in one way or another, unlocking your greatest reward and are ready to find the open door – the one that remains open for as long as you keep it open.

At door number 31 you find the door is unlike the rest, it requires a palm print to open. Go ahead, in your mind imagine holding your palm to the scanner, unlocking an opening the 32st door. By opening this door you have a new freedom, a new hope and all of the power you need to enter into a new chapter of life.

Are you ready?

The 32nd door. But unlike the rest, the door is open, all you need to do is walk through it. Go ahead, walk through the doorway and discover that this is your open door – a new chapter of life as a non-smoker – never looking back and never needing to face those closed doors again. It was worth it to open them, passing through each, making new discoveries, but now you have an open door and the possibilities are limitless.

What can you do with your newfound life? How can you discover how your experience can help others? Or how can you rediscover your true unlimited potential. New health, new wealth and new opportunities await you at every level now and forevermore.

The end of this session is only the beginning. No matter what you have experienced to this point to become a non-smoker, the learning and the process has had value. It has shaped you and moved you and brought you to this point where you have been good to yourself in every way.

Congratulations. It feels great to be a non-smoker, and to have found the open door after searching for so long.

In a moment I am going to ask you to open your eyes, not yet, but in a moment.

first, return your awareness to my voice, to this breath and this moment. To feel the chair where you sit and to be mindfully present. This moment, this breath.

Now pay attention to how you feel. Relaxed but energized, still but hopeful! Begin to stretch any muscles that need to be stretched, you can move your fingers and toes and even gently move your head. Feel the air in the room around you, hear my voice and be ready when I count to three to open the eyes- feeling fantastic and ready for the rest of the day.

1 - paying attention to this breath.

2 - Taking in an energizing deep breath

and 3 opening the eyes, opening the eyes, feeling ready for the rest of the day.

If your eyes are not open yet open the eyes. be present and enjoy the experience of the new you, a non-smoker who has made a lasting decision.

SCALE UP YOUR PRACTICE: FOOLPROOF SYSTEMS TO ATTRACT PREMIUM HYPNOSIS CLIENTS.
With Dr. Richard Nongard and Jason Linett

MONDAY, FEBRUARY 25   9:00AM-5:00PM

In this all-day learning event, you will reach new levels of success and learn to fill every hour in your schedule using the proven techniques that we have used to create thriving practices. We will show you how to launch premium services, and packages, to increase your retention and revenue while providing valued services. You will learn exactly what we have done to build thriving practices and attract new clients, from the ground up.

25 EXPERT LEVEL SPEAKERS SHARING THE EXACT TOOLS THEY USE TO CREATE THERAPEUTIC SUCCESS
Two full days packed with approved continuing education that will change your client outcomes

TUESDAY AND WEDNESDAY, FEBRUARY 26-27, 2019   8AM-6PM EACH DAY

We have hand-picked the highest rated speakers, with the most practical ideas and innovative approaches. We want you to leave this conference not only having had a great time, but also maximizing your potential as a passionate hypnotherapist.

LOCATION: THE ORLEANS HOTEL IN LAS VEGAS

Meals and rooms are not included in your registration. You can get room rates as low as $46 per night (Plus resort fee).

The 2019 H.P.T.I. HypnoConference is open to everyone, but focuses solely on medical hypnotherapy, the business of hypnosis practice, and the real methods that help people make lasting change. If you are passionate about being a skilled helper, and creating a thriving private practice, this conference is for you!

REGISTER NOW AT HPTI.ORG OR BY CALLING (918) 236-6116

THE NEXT STEP!

Now that you have saved your seat, get your hotel reservations! The Orleans is offering the first 100 to book room nights a special discount of $46 per night (plus mandatory resort fee). The Orleans Hotel and

Casino is a landmark hotel in Las Vegas. It is conveniently located near the south end of Las Vegas Blvd. but just off the strip at 4500 W Tropicana Ave. For Reservations call (800) 675-3267 or Register online at https://www.orleanscasino.com/groups and use **group code: A9HWC02**. The Group name is: HPTI Winter Conference. All travel, lodging and meals expenses are the responsibility of attendee and are not included in conference registration/tuition fees.

Questions? Call (918) 236-6116 to Register by Phone or visit HPTI.org to Register Online

www.ingramcontent.com/pod-product-compliance
Lightning Source LLC
Chambersburg PA
CBHW051219250726
48655CB00006B/2493